A-level Study Guide

English Language and Literature

Alan Gardiner

Acknowledgements

Alan Gardiner would like to thank the staff and students of St John Rigby College, Wigan, who have contributed in many ways to the writing of this book.

The publishers are grateful to the following for permission to reproduce copyright material: easyJet for an extract from an advertisement for employment published in *In-flight Magazine* October 2003; Faber & Faber Limited for extracts from *Translations* by Brian Friel and an extract from 'The Trees' from *Collected Poems* by Philip Larkin; Guardian Newspaper Services Limited for 'Inquiries? Now the accent is on profit' by Stephen Khan published in *The Observer*, 24th August 2003 (© Observer), 'It ain't what you do it's the way you say it' by Colin Cottell published in *The Guardian*, 20th December 2003 (© Colin Cottell) and 'Kilroy Silk is an ass. So is the BBC' published in *The Observer*, 11th January 2004 (© Observer); The Labour Party for Tony Blair's speech to the Labour Party Conference 2001 and an extract from Neil Kinnock's 1987 General Election speech at Llandudno; Macmillan Books Limited for an extract from *Bridget Jones's Diary* by Helen Fielding; Methuen Publishing Limited for an extract from *Glengarry Glen Ross* by David Mamet and an extract from *Our Day Out* by Willy Russell; and Mirrorpix/Daily Mirror for an extract from 'Don't give sick Kilroy a platform' published in *The Daily Mirror*, 10th January 2004.

In some instances we have been unable to trace the owners of copyright material and we would appreciate any information that would enable us to do so.

Series Consultants: Geoff Black and Stuart Wall

Pearson Education Limited
Edinburgh Gate, Harlow
Essex CM20 2JE, England
www.pearsoned.co.uk
and Associated Companies throughout the world

© Pearson Education Limited 2005

British Library Cataloguing-in-Publication Data
A catalogue entry for this title is available from the British Library.

ISBN 0-582-77291-5

Set by 35 in Univers, Cheltenham
Printed by Ashford Colour Press, Gosport, Hants

Language terms and concepts

One of the main differences you'll find between your AS/A2 English course and GCSE English is that you're required to look at texts more analytically, and to use more technical terms in doing this. This applies to all the texts that you study, whether it's a Shakespeare play, a transcript of a conversation or an advertisement for a holiday in Ibiza. Students often lose marks in exams because they do not include enough terminology, so you need to develop a familiarity with all the important terms, including – to name a few random examples – 'syndetic listing', 'imperative sentences' and 'ellipsis'. Although these terms often sound difficult, what they actually mean is usually fairly straightforward, so it's really just a case of learning the terms and getting used to using them in your answers.

Another way marks are lost is to name a feature that is in a text (writing something like 'The poet uses a metaphor in line 3'), but to then say nothing about the effect the feature has, or why it is there. So beware of 'feature spotting' – remember you should always add a comment on how the feature relates to the meaning and effect of the text.

This chapter also includes sections on language change. You'll be studying texts from different historical periods, and need to show you can recognise how language has altered over the centuries.

Exam themes

→ Language features (lexis, grammar etc.).

→ How language has changed over time.

Topic checklist

O AS ● A2	OCR	EDEXCEL	AQA A	AQA B	WJEC
Word classes	O●	O●	O●	O●	O●
Lexis and semantics 1	O●	O●	O●	O●	O●
Lexis and semantics 2	O●	O●	O●	O●	O●
Grammar and syntax 1	O●	O●	O●	O●	O●
Grammar and syntax 2	O●	O●	O●	O●	O●
Phonology, discourse and graphology	O●	O●	O●	O●	O●
Dialects and registers	O●	O●	O●	O●	O●
Language change	O●	O●	O●	O●	O●
Analysing texts from the past	O●	O●	O●	O●	O●

Word classes

You were probably taught **word classes** before you started your AS course (possibly even at primary school!), but you may well have forgotten them. Try to learn them early in the course and get into the habit of using them regularly.

Nouns

Nouns are naming words. They are words that give names to people, objects, places, feelings etc. These words all are nouns: *woman*, *pencil*, *Liverpool*, *excitement*.

The main **types of noun** include:

→ **Proper nouns**   These usually begin with a capital letter and refer to specific people, places, occasions etc.: *Italy*, *Olivia*, *Saturday*.

→ **Common nouns**   These are not so specific and refer to types of people, objects, feelings etc.: *student*, *city*, *disappointment*. Most nouns are common nouns, which can be subdivided further into:

→ **Concrete nouns**, which refer to things that physically exist: *house*, *tree*, *table*.

→ **Abstract nouns**, which refer to feelings, ideas, qualities etc. (things that do not physically exist): *freedom*, *friendship*, *strength*.

→ **Collective nouns**, which are names given to groups of people, animals, objects: *team*, *flock*, *herd*.

Adjectives

Adjectives are words used to describe nouns: *an <u>expensive</u> car*, *a <u>tall</u> man*. Words such as *colder* and *bigger* are known as **comparative adjectives** (or simply **comparatives**). Words such as *coldest* and *biggest* are **superlative adjectives** (or simply **superlatives**).

Verbs

Many **verbs** refer to physical actions: *run*, *jump*, *walk* etc. However, they can also refer to 'mental actions' (*think*, *feel*, *imagine*) and to 'states' (*The house <u>stands</u> on a hill*, *That <u>seems</u> fair*). It is also important to remember that *to be* is a verb, as are all its forms (*is*, *was*, *are*, *were* etc.).

The **main verb** in a clause or sentence is a single verb that expresses the main meaning. **Auxiliary verbs** are 'helping' verbs placed in front of main verbs: *I <u>must have been</u> going in the wrong direction*. Here *going* is the main verb. *Must*, *have* and *been* are all being used as auxiliary verbs.

Verbs can also be **active** or **passive**. When a verb is used actively, the person or thing performing the action is emphasised as the subject of the verb: *The teacher <u>spoke</u> to the student*. If the passive voice is used, the emphasis shifts to the object of the verb (the person or thing to which something has been done): *The student <u>was spoken to</u> by the teacher*.

Checkpoint 1

The same word can be a different word class if it is used in different ways. What word class is the word *paint* in each of the following?
→ *She likes to <u>paint</u> in the evening.*
→ *He bought a tin of <u>paint</u>.*

The jargon

Words that clearly refer to actions (*push*, *throw* etc.) are known as **dynamic verbs**. Verbs that refer to states or processes (e.g. *believe*, *know*) are **stative verbs**.

Take note

Primary verbs are verbs that can act as auxiliary verbs and also as main verbs. There are only three of them: *be*, *have* and *do*. For example, *have* is used as a main verb in the sentence *I have a new coat*. **Modal auxiliaries** are only ever used alongside a main verb. There are nine of them: *can*, *could*, *will*, *would*, *shall*, *should*, *may*, *might*, *must*.

Adverbs

Adverbs usually give us more information about verbs, describing verbs in rather the same way that adjectives describe nouns: *She felt better*, *He laughed loudly*. Many adverbs are formed by adding *-ly* to the end of adjectives.

Pronouns

Pronouns are words that take the place of nouns. If the sentence *John gave his telephone number to Laura* is changed to *He gave it to her*, three pronouns take the place of nouns. Many pronouns are **personal pronouns** (pronouns which replace the subject or object of a sentence). They include: *I, me, we, us* (all **first person** pronouns); *you* (**second person**); *he, she, it, him, her, they, them* (**third person**). Other pronouns include such words as *mine, ours, yourself, who, whose, someone, anything*.

Conjunctions

Conjunctions are joining words, used to connect the different parts of a sentence. **Co-ordinating conjunctions** are used when the parts of a sentence are of equal value. The most common are *and, but* and *or* (e.g. *I went to the shop and bought some chocolate*). **Subordinating conjunctions** link a subordinate clause (see page 12) to a main clause. Examples include *because, although, unless, until*.

Prepositions

Prepositions usually indicate in some way how one thing is related to something else. Examples include prepositions relating to position (*on, under, above*), direction (*towards, past, to*) and time (*before, during, after*).

Determiners

Determiners are placed in front of nouns to indicate quantity or identify the noun in some way. The most common are the words *a, an* and *the*. Other examples include *some* (*some money*), *that* (*that car*) and *one, two, three* etc. Most determiners are also a kind of adjective.

Take note

Tense is another important aspect of verbs. Verbs can be **present** (*I am watching television, I watch television frequently*) or **past** (*I watched television last night*). The term *tense* refers to verb endings, which means that strictly speaking English does not have a **future tense** (because we do not attach special endings to verbs to give them a future meaning). Instead we use other kinds of constructions to refer to the future, the most common of which is adding the modal auxiliary *will* or *shall* to the infinitive form of the verb (*I will watch less television once term starts*).

Checkpoint 2

An **intensifier** is a particular kind of adverb. Do you know what this term means, and can you give any examples?

The jargon

Relative pronouns are like other pronouns in that they refer to nouns, but they do not actually take the place of them. They act as linking words in a sentence and are always placed immediately after the noun they refer to: *the man who robbed the bank, a house that has many attractive features*.

Exam preparation (10 minutes)   answer: page 22

Find ten verbs in the following extract from the novel *Wuthering Heights*:

> On that bleak hill-top the earth was hard with a black frost, and the air made me shiver through every limb. Being unable to remove the chain, I jumped over, and, running up the flagged causeway bordered with straggling gooseberry bushes, knocked vainly for admittance, till my knuckles tingled and the dogs howled.

Early Modern English (1450–1700) ●●●

During the **Early Modern English** period English became increasingly **standardised**. William Caxton introduced printing to England in 1476, and this was a crucial factor in the emergence of an accepted 'standard' English. During the Middle English period there were five main regional dialects, each very different from the other. Caxton chose to use the **East Midland dialect** for the texts that he printed (the East Midland area included London, Oxford and Cambridge), and this became established as the most prestigious form of English.

With the arrival of printing, **spelling** and **punctuation** slowly became more standardised. For most of its history English has not had a single, agreed system of spelling. During the Early Modern English period inconsistencies of spelling remained, but gradually became fewer. Most modern punctuation marks entered English after the invention of printing, though it wasn't until the end of this period that something resembling the modern punctuation system began to emerge.

Latin was a strong influence on English **vocabulary** during the 16th and 17th centuries. English had been taking words from Latin for centuries, but during the Renaissance there was an intense interest among scholars in classical texts and authors.

The **grammar** of Early Modern English reflected the fact that this was a time of transition between Middle English and the English we use today. The language of Shakespeare's plays is still marked by unusual **word order**, **archaic inflections** such as -*est* and -*eth*, and the **archaic pronouns** *thou*, *thee* and *thy*.

Late Modern English (1700–present) ●●●

The changes to English since the beginning of the **Late Modern English** period have not been as far reaching as those that occurred in the centuries before. The movement towards a stable, standardised language has continued. Many of the rules of **grammar** that we observe today began life in the 18th century, when several influential textbooks of grammar were written. The first great dictionary of English, compiled by Samuel Johnson, was published in 1755. This made an important contribution to the standardisation of **word meanings** and **spellings**. **Regional differences** in the way language is used have also lessened.

New words have continued to pour into the language. Industrial and technological development, **borrowings** from overseas (especially in recent years from the USA) and changing social and political ideas and attitudes have been the main sources for the additions to our vocabulary.

Links

Standard English (see page 16) evolved from the East Midland dialect.

Take note

The main **phonological** development during the Early Modern English period was the **great vowel shift** of the 15th and 16th centuries, when the pronunciation of long vowel sounds was transformed and became similar to the pronunciation we have today.

Take note

If Latin words that entered the language via French are included, more than half of our modern English vocabulary can be said to be derived from Latin. Latin words are often quite lengthy, and **Latinate vocabulary** tends to sound weighty and learned. Examples include *magnificent*, *ambiguous* and *ultimate*.

Links

For more on Shakespeare's language, see pages 120–125.

Checkpoint 1

Can you think of three reasons why regional differences in language use have decreased?

Checkpoint 2

List some examples to illustrate how these factors have brought new words and expressions into English.

Exam preparation (15 minutes) answer: page 23

With the help of a good dictionary, investigate the origins of the following words: *courtesy, exaggerate, citizen, amusement, anger, ill, romance, belittle, quotation, movie.*

Analysing texts from the past

This section offers advice on analysing short texts from the past (such as poems and prose extracts), though many of the points are also relevant to longer texts. It focuses on linguistic features, but remember that as with all parts of the course your primary concern should always be the **meaning** of a text, and what the writer or speaker is trying to convey.

Periods of English

Remember the periods of English: **Old English** (400–1150); **Middle English** (1150–1450); **Early Modern English** (1450–1700); **Late Modern English** (1700–present).

Identifying the period a text comes from is a useful way to begin an analysis of it. You might also be able to recognise in the text features that are characteristic of the period (see pages 18–19).

Spelling

This may not be relevant to all texts because the spelling may have been modernised, or the text may not be old enough for the spelling to differ from contemporary English.

If it *is* relevant, you should look for **patterns** in the spelling, and try to offer comments and explanations. Common spelling features include:

→ **Extra 'e' at the ends of words**   This usually reflects older pronunciation; also printers sometimes added extra letters to justify text (fill a line).
→ **Doubling of consonants** (as in *travell*)   Unnecessary consonants have fallen away over the centuries; the above point about printing is also sometimes an explanation for double consonants.
→ **y and *i/u* and *v* used in a reverse way to contemporary English**   This occurred before the use of these letters became standardised into the contemporary pattern.

Look also for **inconsistencies** of spelling within a single text. This shows that spelling had not yet become standardised.

Lexis

Vocabulary is often **more formal** in older texts. In addition, look for:

→ **Archaisms**: words/expressions that have disappeared from the language, or are now used only rarely.
→ **Archaic meanings**: words/expressions where the meaning has changed (e.g. **narrowing** or **broadening** may have occurred).
→ **Archaic contractions** (e.g. *'tis*).
→ If you are comparing texts, words/expressions in the later text that are **unlikely to have existed at the time of the older text** (e.g. **neologisms**, modern colloquialisms, words referring to modern inventions etc.).
→ Vocabulary that reflects **social and cultural change** (e.g. the influence of political correctness in later texts).

Grammar

Sentences are often **longer** and **more complex** in older texts. In addition, look for:

→ **Archaic inflections** (e.g. *ha<u>th</u>*, *did<u>st</u>*).
→ **Archaic pronouns** (e.g. *thee*, *thy*).
→ Differences in **word order**, and constructions that would be unlikely to occur in contemporary English.
→ **Archaic verb forms** (e.g. *art* for *are*).
→ Differences in the formation of: **the past tense/negatives/plurals/ interrogatives**.
→ **Punctuation** differences (e.g. more frequent use of colons).

Checkpoint 2

What are **interrogatives**?

Phonology

→ Older **pronunciation** may be reflected in the spelling of words.
→ Some older texts (e.g. the Authorised Version of the Bible) were intended to be **read aloud**, and the language used may reflect this.

Discourse structure/graphology

→ The **organisation** of the text may reflect the age of the text in some way (e.g. newspaper articles in the past tended to have longer paragraphs).
→ There may be old-fashioned **graphological features** (e.g. font styles).

Exam preparation (30 minutes)   answer: page 23

The text below is an extract from one of a series of letters written by Lady Brilliana Harley in the years 1625–1643. The letter is to her husband, Sir Robert Harley. In what ways does the language used in the letter differ from present-day English?

> Deare Sr – Your two leters, on from Hearifort and the other from Gloster, weare uery wellcome to me: and if you knwe howe gladly I reseaue your leters, I beleeue you would neeuer let any opertunity pase. I hope your cloche did you saruis betwne Gloster and my brother Brays, for with vs it was a very rainy day, but this day has bine very dry and warme, and so I hope it was with you; and to-morowe I hope you will be well at your journis end, wheare I wisch my self to bide you wellcome home. You see howe my thoughts goo with you: and as you haue many of mine, so let me haue some of yours. Beleeue me, I thinke I neuer miste you more then nowe I doo, or ells I haue forgoot what is past. I thanke God, Ned and Robin are well; and Ned askes every day wheare you are, and he says you will come to-morowe. My father is well, but goos not abrode, because of his fiseke*.

Examiner's secrets

The main aspects of language to look at here are spelling, lexis and grammar.

Take note

* *fiseke*: medical treatment ('physic').

21

Answers
Language terms and concepts

Word classes

Checkpoints

1 In the first sentence *paint* is a verb. In the second it is a noun.
2 An intensifier is a word that increases or decreases the intensity of another word or phrase. Examples include *really, very, hardly, scarcely*.

Exam preparation

Ten verbs in the extract: *was, made, shiver, Being, remove, jumped, running, knocked, tingled, howled*.

Lexis and semantics 1

Checkpoints

1 An extended metaphor is a metaphorical comparison that is developed and extended, for example over several lines of a poem.
2 Hyponyms of *poem* include *sonnet, ode, elegy, limerick* and so on.

Exam preparation

Used literally, the words listed would actually refer to parts of the body, as in *He used his foot to prevent me closing the door*. In the following sentences the words are used figuratively:
He agreed to foot the bill.
The house overlooked the mouth of the river.
You'll have to take it on the chin.
We see eye to eye on most things.
The president hadn't the stomach for another war.
His friends said he was under her thumb.
We must face facts.
I'm not going to shoulder the blame for this.
The dispute was coming to a head.
It cost me an arm and a leg.
Now we're getting to the heart of the matter.
The two teams are neck and neck in the championship race.

Lexis and semantics 2

Checkpoints

1 The play on words is based on the idea of spreading butter. Another linguistic feature of the headline is alliteration.
2 Bathos is the sense of comic anticlimax created when a literary work drops from an elevated or serious level to the absurd or ridiculous.

Exam preparation

The pairs are as follows (less formal word first):
chopper–helicopter; scarper–retreat; quiz–interrogate; drink–beverage; cop–police officer; chat–converse; brief–barrister; broke–impecunious; binmen–refuse collectors; job–occupation.

Grammar and syntax 1

Checkpoints

1 Auxiliary verbs are 'helping' verbs placed in front of main verbs, as in *I might see you tomorrow*. See page 4.
2 No. For example, the adverbial in the specimen sentence on page 10 could be moved to the beginning of the sentence: *Yesterday a visitor called the old house a ruin*.

Exam preparation

The noun phrases are: *She; He; his eyes; John; Mark; a key; Paula; The crowd; her; Leaves; the trees; Fiona; the money; her purse*. Examples of how some of these phrases could be extended by adding pre-modifiers or post-modifiers: *his tired eyes; a key attached to a red ribbon*.

Grammar and syntax 2

Checkpoints

1 Declarative – because it is a statement rather than a direct command.
2 The heavily syndetic listing emphasises the great abundance of food.

Exam preparation

Examples of the effects these kinds of sentences might be used to achieve: short, simple sentences – to create a sense of tension; long, complex sentence – to describe something happening slowly; declarative – to give information; interrogative – to suggest the narrator's doubts or uncertainties; imperative – to speak directly to the reader; exclamatory – to convey surprise or enthusiasm.

Phonology, discourse and graphology

Checkpoints

1 Onomatopoeia occurs when the sound of a word echoes its meaning (e.g. *splash*). Alliteration occurs when two or more words begin with the same sound (but not always the same letter).
2 Antonyms.

Exam preparation

Cohesive devices include: repetition (especially of *struggle, domination, ideal*); anaphoric references (*This, this struggle, It*); conjunctions (*then, But, and*).

Dialects and registers

Checkpoints

1 The Received Pronunciation (or RP) accent. This is the accent associated with educated, upper-class speakers of English.

2 The level of formality might well differ when speaking with friends rather than strangers. This might also be true when writing a letter rather than an essay, though this would depend on the type of letter and the recipient. Letters and essays also have different conventions of layout and structure.

Exam preparation

The register here is that of a newspaper sports report rather than a natural conversation. This is especially evident in the lexis, which includes a large amount of journalese (words and phrases that are especially common in newspapers). Examples include *shock FA Cup exit*, *Plucky Tranmere*, *a three-goal deficit*, *another Premiership scalp*, *the stuff of FA Cup legend*, *their lowly league placing*, *the in-form Reds*. None of these noun phrases is likely to occur in normal everyday speech. The contrived phonological effects – specifically, the use of alliteration – are also associated with newspapers rather than natural speech: *Terrific Tranmere*, *KO the Kop Kings*.

Language change

Checkpoints

1 Three important reasons are: the growth in education; movement of people around the country; the effects of the mass media.
2 Technological developments have brought in words such as *internet*, *online*, *texting*, *cyberspace* and so on. Borrowings from the USA include *chill out*, *pass the buck*, *sidetracked*. Changing ideas and attitudes have introduced words and phrases such as *ageism*, *grey power*, *pester power*.

Exam preparation

Word origins are shown in brackets: courtesy (French); exaggerate (Latin); citizen (French); amusement (French); anger (Old Norse); ill (Old Norse); romance (French); belittle (American); quotation (Latin); movie (American).

Analysing texts from the past

Checkpoints

1 The avoidance of language that might cause offence to particular minority groups.
2 Questions.

Exam preparation

This text is from the Early Modern English period and has several of the features associated with the language of that time.

There are numerous instances where the spelling of individual words differs from that found in contemporary English. Many words have an extra *e* ending: *deare*, *howe*, *warme*, *thinke* and so on. These endings are common in the English of the period. Also characteristic is the use of the letter *u* where now there would be *v*: *uery*. At the same time, there is a reverse pattern in the spelling of the time, with *v* instead of *u* at the beginning of words: *vs*. Use of *i* and *y* had not yet settled into the present English pattern, and this is reflected in the spelling of *journis*.

A feature of the punctuation of the period – reflected in this text – is that there was much more extensive use of the semi-colon than in contemporary English, used where we would have full stops or commas. Another feature of the time is that an apostrophe followed by an *s* is not used to show possession: this is evident in *your journis end*.

The vocabulary includes archaic words that have since passed out of use: *fiseke*. There are also expressions that are now obsolete or at least rarely heard: *did you saruis*, *goos not abrode*, *bide you wellcome home*.

In terms of grammar, many of the constructions used are similar to those found in contemporary English. Occasionally the word order is different: *more than nowe I do* instead of *more than I do now*. There are also constructions that would seem awkward and unnatural today: *or ells I haue forgoot what is past*. Verb endings are not always the same as in contemporary English: *miste* is used for *missed*.

→ Using appropriate forms of address.

→ Speaking to others in a way that is appropriate to the social relationship you have with them.

→ Speaking with a degree of formality appropriate to the occasion.

→ Understanding the conventions of language associated with particular situations (e.g. accepting or refusing an invitation, beginning and ending a conversation).

→ Understanding the conventions of turn taking.

Robin Lakoff (1973) argued that much conversational interaction is governed by what she called the **politeness principle**. **Brown and Levinson** (1987) speak of face needs being met by positive and negative politeness. **Positive politeness** is demonstrated when we show people that they are liked and admired. **Negative politeness** is shown when we avoid intruding on others' lives, taking care not to impose our presence on them or pry into their personal affairs.

Gender ●●●

An important aspect of the study of conversation is the question of **gender difference** in conversational behaviour. Researchers have found that women tend to be more supportive in their conversational behaviour than men. In essence, women's approach to conversation tends to be **co-operative**, whereas men's approach tends to be **competitive**.

Specifically, women tend to:

→ Ask more questions (showing interest in what other speakers think, and encouraging them to participate).

→ Give more supportive feedback when listening (e.g. through oral signals such as *mm* and through expressions of agreement and understanding such as *I know*, *Yes* etc.).

→ Pay more compliments.

→ Initiate more topics of conversation.

→ Make more effort to bring others into the conversation.

→ Use *you* and *we* more often (i.e. they address others more and involve them more in what is being said).

→ Develop the ideas of previous speakers more than men do.

In contrast, men are more likely to:

→ Interrupt.

→ Express disagreement.

→ Ignore the other person's utterances.

→ Show reluctance to pursue topics initiated by others.

Watch out!

Researchers have identified trends and tendencies, but many individual men and women do not conform to the expected pattern. It is important not to assume that all men and women are the same!

Take note

Researchers have also investigated what men and women talk about. Women's conversation often relates to personal experiences, relationships and family issues. Male conversation tends to focus more on information, facts, objects and activities. Again, it is important not to over-generalise: these findings do not apply to all men or all women, nor to all conversations.

Take note

Another research finding is that women's speech tends to be closer to Standard English than men's.

Take note

Some specifications require a coursework assignment that investigates spoken language. Transcripts that enable you to comment on gender can be useful for this.

Exam preparation   answer: page 47

Record a few short snippets of conversation (no more than about 60 seconds each), involving male and female friends. Do the conversations support the view that there are gender differences in conversational behaviour?

Prepared talk: speeches 1

The jargon

The techniques used by speakers to make their speeches powerful and persuasive are known as **rhetorical features**.

Public speeches are one of the main forms of spoken language studied at AS and A2. This first section on speeches looks at some important grammatical features associated with speeches.

Grammatical features

Parallelism

Parallelism involves the use of phrases, clauses or sentences with a similar grammatical structure. Earl Spencer began his speech at the funeral of his sister, Diana Princess of Wales, with the following sentence:

> I stand before you today the representative of a family in grief, in a country in mourning, before a world in shock.

Here the parallel phrases are *a family in grief*, *a country in mourning* and *a world in shock*. Parallelism helps to create a strong, emphatic rhythm, and it can be used to stress key ideas. In this example, the extent of the grief caused by Diana's death is emphasised (note the progression from *family* to *country* to *world*).

Repetition

This can be of single words or of complete phrases or sentences. As with parallelism, the effect is often to emphasise important words or ideas and to create a powerful rhythm. Repetition can give a speech **cohesion**, as in the famous Martin Luther King speech where he repeated the words *I have a dream*. A simpler example of repetition is Tony Blair's declaration that the priorities of his government were *Education, education, education*.

The jargon

The term **cohesion** refers to the techniques used to connect different parts of a text with each other.

Contrast and antithesis

A balanced rhythm is created by the use of words and phrases that contrast in some way. Antithesis is an especially powerful kind of contrast, as the words involved have directly opposite meanings. This quotation is from Abraham Lincoln's address at the Gettysburg military cemetery in 1863:

> The brave men living and dead, who struggled here, have consecrated it far above our power to add or detract. The world will little note, nor long remember what we say here, but it can never forget what they did here.

Note the series of contrasts here: *living–dead*; *add–detract*; *little–long*; *remember–forget*; *what we say here–what they did here*.

Take note

Parallelism is also present here: *little note – long remember, remember what we say here – forget what they did here.*

Tripling

Three-part lists (also known as **sets of three**) have a memorable rhythm and often feature in speeches. The earlier quotation from Earl Spencer is an example. In a wartime speech Winston Churchill referred to *blood, toil, tears and sweat*. This is a four-part list, but over the years it has become a well-known expression, modified to the more easily remembered set of three: *blood, sweat and tears*.

Listing

Lists have a cumulative effect, and are often used to reinforce an idea or argument. In a speech in October 2001, delivered a few weeks after the September 11th terrorist attack on the World Trade Centre in New York, President Bush used listing to emphasise the strength and solidarity of the American response:

> Our nation is grateful to so many Americans who are rallying to our cause and preparing for the struggle ahead: FBI agents, intelligence officers, emergency response workers, public health authorities, state and local officials, our diplomats abroad, law enforcement teams who safeguard our security at home, and soldiers, sailors, marines and airmen who defend us so far away.

Sentence length

Sentences in speeches are often notable for being short, direct and powerful. Alternatively, long sentences which build to a climax may be present (they are especially common towards the ends of speeches). Abraham Lincoln's Gettysburg address ended with the following climactic sentence:

> It is rather for us to be here dedicated to the great task remaining before us – that from these honoured dead we take increased devotion to that cause for which they gave the last full measure of devotion – that we here highly resolve that these dead shall not have died in vain – that this nation, under God, shall have a new birth of freedom – and that government of the people, by the people, for the people, shall not perish from the earth.

Use of first and second person

The use of first person plural pronouns (*we, our*) promotes a feeling of unity and solidarity between speaker and audience. Second person pronouns (*you, your*) involve the audience by addressing them directly.

Interrogatives

Asking questions is another way of involving the audience, though usually of course they are not expected to answer them. A question may be answered by the speaker: *And what has the government done about it? Nothing!* Alternatively, it may be a **rhetorical question** – that is, a question that does not require an answer (usually because the answer is obvious). Asking a question requires a change in intonation, so questions make the delivery of a speech more varied and dynamic.

Checkpoint 1

What is the difference between **syndetic** and **asyndetic listing**?

Checkpoint 2

What other **rhetorical features** can you identify in this extract?

Example

In Martin Luther King's *I have a dream* speech, the repeated use of first person plural pronouns shows that King identifies with his audience, and also stresses that they are united in a common cause:

> In the process of gaining our rightful place we must not be guilty of wrongful deeds. Let us not seek to satisfy our thirst for freedom by drinking from the cup of bitterness and hatred. We must forever conduct our struggle on the high plane of dignity and discipline.

Exam preparation   answer: page 47

See page 41 for a practice question relevant to this and the following section.

Prepared talk: speeches 2

We now consider the lexical and phonological aspects of speeches. There is also a practice question on a Tony Blair speech.

Lexical features

Simple vocabulary

Simple, possibly **monosyllabic** vocabulary may be used in order to be clear, direct and forceful. However, speeches can also employ **elaborate**, **elevated vocabulary** to add solemnity and weight to a speech, or to make it sound dramatic and uplifting.

Checkpoint 1

Explain the difference between **monosyllabic** and **polysyllabic** vocabulary.

Emotive vocabulary

Vocabulary intended to stir the emotions of the audience is common in speeches. In a speech early in the Second World War, Churchill used emotive language to stress the iniquity of Nazi Germany:

> Side by side, the British and French peoples have advanced to rescue not only Europe but mankind from the foulest and most soul-destroying tyranny which has ever darkened and stained the pages of history.

Checkpoint 2

Which words and phrases in this extract are especially emotive?

Hyperbole

This is the use of exaggeration. Again it is often used for emotive effect, or for dramatic impact. In a powerful speech during the General Election of 1987, the Labour Party leader Neil Kinnock spoke of the battle during the 20th century to eradicate privilege and secure equality of opportunity for ordinary people ('Glenys' is a reference to his wife):

> Why am I the first Kinnock in a thousand generations to be able to get to university? Why is Glenys the first woman in her family in a thousand generations to be able to get to university?

Taken literally, this implies that universities have existed for *a thousand generations* – which, of course, they haven't.

Figurative language

Metaphors and **similes** can make a speech more vivid and memorable. Martin Luther King's *I have a dream* speech makes extensive use of figurative language. He says that the abolition of slavery in the USA was *a joyous daybreak to end the long night of captivity*. However, one hundred years later black Americans still inhabited *a lonely island of poverty in the middle of a vast ocean of material prosperity*.

Phonology

If you are analysing a speech, never forget that it is intended to be *heard*. This means **sound** and **rhythm** are especially important. Consider the rhythm of specific parts of the speech (e.g. stress on particular words) and of the speech as a whole. As was noted, several of the grammatical features listed in the previous section (pages 38–39) have a rhythmic effect. Look also for phonological devices such as **alliteration**, **assonance** and **rhyme**.

Links

For more on phonological devices such as alliteration and assonance, see page 65.

Checkpoint 3

Before beginning your answer to this question, answer the following as fully as possible: who are the audience for this speech?

Exam preparation (45 minutes)   answer: page 47

The text below is the beginning of a speech given by Prime Minister Tony Blair at the Labour Party Conference in 2001. The speech was delivered a few weeks after the September 11th terrorist attacks on New York. Comment on the language of the speech, focusing in particular on Blair's use of rhetorical techniques associated with public speeches.

Conference, in retrospect the millennium marked a moment in time, but it was the events of the 11 September that marked a turning point in history. When we confront the dangers of the future and assess the choices facing human kind. It was a tragedy, an act of evil and from this nation goes our deepest sympathy and prayers for the victims and our profound solidarity with the American people. We were with you at the first, we will stay with you to the last . . .

Just two weeks ago in New York after the church service I met some of the families of the British victims, and it was in many ways a very British occasion, tea and biscuits, raining outside and around the edge of the room strangers making small talk, trying to be normal people, in a very abnormal situation. And as you crossed the room you felt the longing and the sadness. Hands that were clutching photos of sons and daughters, wives and husbands, imploring you to believe that when they said there was still an outside chance of their loved ones being found alive it could be true, when in truth you knew that all hope was gone.

Then a middle aged mother looks you in the eyes and tells you that her only son has died and asks you why, and I tell you, you do not feel like the most powerful man in the country at times like that. Because there is no answer. There is no justification for the pain of those people. Her son did nothing wrong, the woman seven months pregnant whose child will never know its father did nothing wrong. And they don't want revenge. They want something better in memory of their loved ones. And I believe that their memorial can and should be greater than simply the punishment of the guilty. It is that out of the shadow of this evil should emerge lasting good. Destruction of the machinery of terrorism wherever it is found, hope amongst all nations of a new beginning where we seek to resolve differences in a calm and ordered way. Greater understanding between nations and between faiths, and above all, justice and prosperity for the poor and dispossessed so that people everywhere can see the chance of a better future through the hard work and creative power of the free citizen, not the violence and savagery of the fanatic. (This is the Labour Party's transcript of the speech).

of what we would expect). The description of Alison in *The Miller's Tale* begins *Fair was this yonge wyf*, not 'This yonge wyf was fair' (incidentally, note how Chaucer's construction has the advantage of stressing *Fair*). Another grammatical feature of Middle English is that several **inflections** (word endings that serve a grammatical function) were in use that later disappeared from the language. These include *-th* or *-eth* at the ends of verbs (*maketh*, *toucheth*) and *-en* as a verb ending (*slepen*) or to indicate a noun is plural (*eyen* for 'eyes').

Phonology

Sound is especially important in Chaucer's poems because he was working within an **oral** literary tradition. Poetry was generally intended to be read aloud to groups of listeners. As you are reading your text, try to imagine how it would sound when spoken, and look for effects achieved by the sounds of words. If you can, listen to a tape of the text being read in Middle English. Alternatively, many editions of Chaucer's poems include some guidance on pronunciation.

The Canterbury Tales ●●●

The Canterbury Tales consists of stories told by a group of pilgrims who are on their way from London to Canterbury. In the opening poem, *The General Prologue*, the narrator (who identifies himself as one of the pilgrims) gives a description of his companions and explains the proposal for a story-telling competition. Each pilgrim is to tell four stories, two on the outward journey and two as they return. As there are over 30 pilgrims, a complete *Canterbury Tales* would have comprised over 120 tales. In fact Chaucer never completed the work, and there are only 24 tales, spread over an assortment of manuscripts, some containing sequences of several tales, some only one tale.

Chaucer seems to have chosen the situation of a pilgrimage because it enabled him to present a marvellous panorama of medieval life. His pilgrims cover a range of ages, occupations and classes, and their personalities and moral natures are equally varied. This diversity is also reflected in the stories they tell. In most of the poems there is a close relationship between the tale and its teller, and if you are studying one of the tales you will probably find that the **role of the narrator** is a key topic. The portrait of the relevant pilgrim in *The General Prologue* is a good place to start. You then need to look closely at how the tale reflects the pilgrim's attitudes, values and personality.

Checkpoint 2

Give two examples of inflections that still exist in contemporary English.

Take note

With some tales it is also useful to consider how the poem relates to other tales. For example, *The Miller's Tale* immediately follows *The Knight's Tale*, and while there are interesting parallels between the two stories, the contrasts are even more striking.

Exam preparation (45 minutes)

Write an essay examining the character and role of the narrator in the tale that you are studying. Refer closely to Chaucer's use of language in your answer.

Poetic form and structure

Examiner's secrets

Remember your primary focus must always be on the **meaning** of the poem. How does the poet **use** the form of the poem to convey thoughts, feelings and ideas?

Links

Metre and **rhyme** are important aspects of poetic form. See pages 62–65.

Links

For more on the **iambic pentameter**, see page 62.

Checkpoint 1

Name three Romantic poets.

This section is concerned with the overall shape and organisation of poems. The terms **form** and **structure** are often used interchangeably, but form is really a narrower term referring to the kinds of poetry poets use to organise their thoughts and ideas – sonnets, couplets, blank verse and so on. Structure refers to the overall arrangement of a poem. This can include the poem's form, but it also includes such elements as the sequence of ideas (for example, how the poem begins and ends).

Stanzas

A **stanza** is a section of a poem consisting of several lines of verse. Many poems are divided into stanzas of equal length (e.g. three or four lines). Four-line stanzas, known as **quatrains**, are especially common, and are often combined with a regular **metre** and **rhyme scheme**. If a poem is organised into stanzas, you should think about why this is and about the relationship between the stanzas. How does the poem develop as it moves from stanza to stanza? Are there important contrasts between individual stanzas?

Lyric poetry

The majority of poems can be classified as **lyric poetry**. A lyric poem expresses an individual's thoughts and feelings. Lyrics are usually quite short, and the most common subject is love. **Sonnets**, **odes** and **elegies** (see below) are all examples of lyric poetry. Apart from the lyric, the other dominant type of poetry is **narrative poetry** (see opposite page).

Sonnets

A **sonnet** is a poem of 14 lines, with a rhythm usually based on the **iambic pentameter**. The two most common kinds of sonnet are the **Petrarchan** and the **Shakespearean**:

→ The **Petrarchan** sonnet uses a rhyme scheme that divides the poem into two sections, an **octave** (the first eight lines) and a **sestet** (the last six lines). The rhyme scheme is usually *abbaabba*, *cdecde* (or *cdcdcd*).

→ The **Shakespearean** sonnet has three **quatrains** (units of four lines each) and ends with a **couplet** (a pair of rhyming lines). The usual rhyme scheme is *abab*, *cdcd*, *efef*, *gg*.

The sonnet is an Italian form that entered English poetry in the 16th century. The earliest English sonnets were love poems. Love has continued to be the topic most strongly associated with sonnets, but poets have used the form for a great variety of subjects; religious sonnets are also common, and the Romantic poets wrote many sonnets about nature.

If you are analysing a sonnet, you should look closely at the relationship between the different sections of the poem, as the divisions often mark shifts in meaning or attitude. In Petrarchan sonnets, for instance, the octave sometimes outlines a situation or problem, while the sestet offers a response to it. In Shakespearean sonnets, the final couplet may express a concluding thought or introduce a new idea.

Odes

An **ode** is an elaborate lyric poem, often extending over several stanzas, usually addressed to a person, object or idea. Odes are also usually serious poems that praise the person or thing addressed, and meditate upon its qualities. Famous odes include Shelley's *Ode to the West Wind*, Keats's *Ode to Autumn* and Marvell's *Horatian Ode upon Cromwell's Return from Ireland*.

Elegies

An **elegy** is a poem that mourns someone's death, such as Tennyson's *In Memoriam*, which was written in memory of A.H. Hallam, a friend of the poet. The term is also sometimes applied more generally to solemn, contemplative poems. Thomas Gray's famous *Elegy Written in a Country Churchyard* is a reflective poem about death.

Narrative poetry

Narrative poetry is poetry that tells a story. Before novels became popular in the 18th century, stories were usually told in verse, and even after the advent of the novel many poets continued to write narrative verse. The two main forms of narrative poetry are the **epic** and the **ballad**:

→ **Epics** are long poems, often about mythical heroes, and often with grand, impressive settings and elements of the supernatural.
→ **Ballads** tell stories in simple, everyday language. The emphasis is on action and dialogue, with description usually kept to a minimum. Many ballads use the traditional **ballad metre**, which comprises rhyming **quatrains** (four-line stanzas) of alternate four-stress and three-stress lines. Also common is the use of a **refrain** – the regular repetition of words or lines, usually at the end of a stanza.

Links

The *Specimen texts* section on pages 68–69 includes three examples of sonnets.

Examiner's secrets

As well as identifying the form of a poem, consider other elements of its structure. How does it begin, develop and end? Does the structural pattern of the poem change or break down at any point?

Checkpoint 2

An example of an **epic** poem is *Paradise Lost*, a long 17th-century religious poem about the fall of man. Who wrote it?

Exam preparation (30 minutes)   answer: page 70

Text A on page 68 is a sonnet by Shakespeare, *My mistress' eyes are nothing like the sun*. Explore the poet's attitude towards the woman described in this poem, referring closely to his use of language and of the sonnet form.

Poetic imagery

The term **imagery** is sometimes used very broadly to refer to any aspect of a piece of writing that appeals to the reader's senses – a visual description, for example, or a description of a sound or a taste. More narrowly, the term also refers specifically to the use in literature of **comparisons**, especially **similes**, **metaphors** and **personification**. Imagery can occur in any kind of text, but is especially common in poetry.

Figurative and literal language

Literal language means what it says. **Figurative** language is language that is not literally true. If the sentence *He kicked the bucket* refers to someone who lost their temper and kicked over a pail of water, it is literal. If it is a colloquial remark meaning someone died, it is figurative.

In the texts you are studying you will probably encounter a large amount of figurative language. Poets in particular use comparisons to make their writing more vivid, suggestive or precise. When you come across an image, you should ask yourself these questions:

→ What are the two things that are being compared? Here the terms **tenor** and **vehicle** are useful – see **metaphors** below.
→ How are they similar? Often there is more than one similarity.
→ What is conveyed or achieved by the comparison? For example, the comparison may highlight a particular characteristic of the thing that is being described.
→ What is the significance of the comparison in relation to the text as a whole? There may be links with other images in the text, or the comparison may relate in some way to an important theme.

Similes

A **simile** is a comparison that uses the words *like* or *as*. This example is from Wordsworth's *Composed upon Westminster Bridge* (see page 67).

> This City now doth, like a garment, wear
> The beauty of the morning

The simile *like a garment* compares London's early morning splendour to a beautiful piece of clothing. It suggests how the buildings are bathed in sunlight, and also implies that the beauty is transitory, that London is not always as beautiful as this (clothing is not worn all the time).

Checkpoint 1

List five other figurative expressions in everyday use.

Take note

A word or expression that is not meant to be taken literally is also known as a **figure of speech**.

Examiner's secrets

Never simply write, 'There is a metaphor in the third stanza'. Always explain what is being compared, and what the effect or significance of the comparison is.

Metaphors

Whereas a simile acknowledges that the things being compared are separate (by using *like* or *as*), a **metaphor** goes one stage further and describes something as if it actually were something else – what is said is not literally true. In the following extract from the poem *Last Lesson of the Afternoon*, D.H. Lawrence (who briefly worked as a teacher) uses the metaphor of a hunt to describe the situation in a classroom as the school day draws to a close:

> When will the bell ring, and end this weariness?
> How long have they tugged the leash, and strained apart,
> My pack of unruly hounds! I cannot start
> Them again on a quarry of knowledge they hate to hunt,
> I can haul them and urge them no more.

Much of the language here is metaphorical. For example, the pupils are not really a pack of hounds, and they have not been tugging on a leash. The image is effective because the comparison with a hunt works in several different ways. The pupils are like a pack of hunting hounds in that they are noisy and restless. The teacher resembles a huntsman who has the hounds on a leash but is struggling to control them, just as the teacher is struggling to control the class. The pupils are meant to be searching for knowledge, in the same way that hounds are meant to pursue a *quarry* (which might, for example, be a fox). However, the pupils are not interested in the search for knowledge, so that they are like hounds being urged to pursue a quarry *they hate to hunt*.

A metaphor such as this which is introduced and then **developed**, either over several lines (as here) or over a complete text, is called an **extended metaphor**. Two other relevant terms are **tenor** and **vehicle**: the tenor is the subject of the metaphor (in this case, the situation in the classroom), the vehicle is what it is compared with (here, a hunt).

Personification

Personification occurs when something that is not human or alive is described as if it were. The earlier quotation from *Composed upon Westminster Bridge* is an example of personification, because London is compared to someone wearing a garment. There is more personification elsewhere in the poem:

> Dear God! the very houses seem asleep,
> And all that mighty heart is lying still!

Checkpoint 2

Comment on the effectiveness of the verbs in this extract.

The jargon

There are also terms for the ways that images appeal to our senses:
- → a **visual** image appeals to our sense of sight;
- → an **auditory** (or aural) image appeals to our sense of hearing;
- → a **tactile** image appeals to our sense of touch;
- → an **olfactory** image appeals to our sense of smell;
- → a **gustatory** image appeals to our sense of taste.

Watch out!

The term **tenor** can also mean 'register'.

Exam preparation (30 minutes)   answer: page 70

Text B on page 68 is *Holy Sonnet XIV*, written by the Metaphysical poet John Donne (see page 50). Examine Donne's use of imagery in this poem.

Prose fiction

This chapter looks at the features of novels and short stories. You are likely to be studying a prose fiction set text, but also need to be prepared in the exam to analyse extracts from prose fiction texts you have not read before. With some specifications the way **dialogue** is presented in fiction is especially important, and you need to consider the stylistic features of fictional dialogue and how it differs from real-life conversation. **Plot**, **narrative viewpoint**, **characters** and **themes** are other important aspects. As with all kinds of texts, you will also be expected to analyse closely the ways writers of prose fiction use language.

Exam themes

→ Literary and linguistic features of prose fiction texts.

→ Dialogue in novels and short stories.

→ Characters and themes.

→ Prose fiction texts of different periods.

Topic checklist

○ AS ● A2	OCR	EDEXCEL	AQA A	AQA B	WJEC
Historical overview	○●	○●	○●	○●	○●
Plot and setting	○●	○●	○●	○●	○●
Narrative viewpoint	○●	○●	○●	○●	○●
Characters and themes	○●	○●	○●	○●	○●
Dialogue in prose fiction	○●	○●	○●	○●	○●
Lexis and imagery	○●	○●	○●	○●	○●
Grammar and phonology	○●	○●	○●	○●	○●
Analysing prose fiction extracts	○●	○●	○●	○●	○●
Specimen texts	○●	○●	○●	○●	○●

Historical overview

Before the 18th century, drama and poetry were the dominant forms of literature. The tremendous growth in the popularity of the novel since then (especially in the 19th and 20th centuries) has meant that it has become the leading modern literary form. This section identifies some important developments and some major authors in the history of prose fiction.

18th century

Although there are earlier forms of writing that can be seen as antecedents of the novel, the first true English novels appeared in the early 18th century, notably **Daniel Defoe**'s *Robinson Crusoe* and *Moll Flanders*. The other major 18th-century novelists, who came after Defoe, were **Samuel Richardson**, **Henry Fielding** and **Laurence Sterne**.

19th century

The 19th century, especially the middle decades, is regarded as the great age of the novel. The major novels of the period are generally characterised by a combination of **psychological complexity** and **social realism**. They explore the morality and emotional life of individual characters, while also addressing broader contemporary issues such as the effects of the Industrial Revolution and of social class divisions. Important authors include:

→ **Jane Austen**   Austen's novels typically focus on the dilemmas of upper-class young women, torn between the expectations of society and the promptings of their own moral conscience. Her books remain popular today, celebrated for their social comedy and astute, ironic observation. Austen's novels include *Pride and Prejudice*, *Emma* and *Mansfield Park*.

→ **Charles Dickens**   Dickens was enormously popular in his own lifetime, in Britain and the USA. His novels are notable for their memorable characters and exposure of the injustices and corruption of 19th-century society. Dickens's many works include *Great Expectations*, *Hard Times*, *David Copperfield* and *Bleak House*.

→ **Emily Brontë**   *Wuthering Heights* was Emily Brontë's only novel, and was only recognised as a masterpiece after her death. Emily was one of the Brontë sisters. **Anne** wrote *The Tenant of Wildfell Hall* and *Agnes Grey*. **Charlotte's** major novels were *Jane Eyre* and *Villette*.

→ **Thomas Hardy**   Hardy's novels appeared later in the century. They show an interest in rural life (they are usually set in Hardy's native West Country), and a sympathy for characters who rebel against social conventions. The lives of his central characters often follow a tragic pattern, their downfall demonstrating the power of fate. *Tess of the D'Urbevilles*, *Far From the Madding Crowd* and *The Mayor of Casterbridge* are among Hardy's novels.

Take note

Samuel Richardson wrote **epistolary** novels, where the story is told through letters written by the major characters. Fielding's works (such as *Joseph Andrews* and *Tom Jones*) are comic, and closer in form to the modern novel. In particular, he made use of an **intrusive omniscient narrator**, a device discussed on page 79.

Checkpoint 1

Other important 19th-century novelists include: **George Eliot**, **Anthony Trollope**, **W.M. Thackeray**, **Elizabeth Gaskell** and **Henry James**. Can you name any of their books?

Checkpoint 2

Can you name any of **Charles Dickens's** other works?

Take note

Wuthering Heights tells of the doomed, passionate relationship between Catherine Earnshaw and the mysterious Heathcliff. Catherine decides, disastrously, to marry for social advantage. The novel explores Catherine's motives and the consequences of her action, and vividly evokes the wild Yorkshire moors that are the story's setting.

20th century

The tendency for the novel to focus on the individual consciousness increased in the 20th century. Many modern novels have heroes who are **alienated**, unable to connect with the world around them. 19th-century novels were **realist** in their approach, in that they generally sought to make the reader believe in a fictional world. This tradition has continued to the present day, but during the 20th century there were also many novelists who were more **experimental** in their approach. Instead of trying to hide the fact that they were writing fiction, they drew attention to the novel as a constructed work of art, and to their own role as author, by playing with different narrative voices, mixing genres and incorporating unexpected time-shifts.

Important 20th-century writers include:

→ **Joseph Conrad** Conrad came to Britain as a Polish sailor, and many of his novels and short stories are based on his experiences at sea. His works are carefully structured and technically sophisticated, often involving the use of a fictional character, Marlow, as narrator. His novels and stories include *Heart of Darkness*, *Nostromo* and *The Secret Agent*.

→ **E.M. Forster** Forster's works often concern the barriers people have to overcome in forming relationships. *A Passage To India* portrays India under British rule, exploring relationships between people of different races. In *A Room With A View* the central characters have to overcome social convention and prejudice to find love.

→ **James Joyce** Joyce was an experimental writer who is especially associated with the **stream of consciousness** technique, which seeks to capture as accurately as possible an individual's flow of thoughts. *Ulysses*, a novel about a day in the life of its central character, is in this tradition. Joyce also wrote the autobiographical novel *A Portrait of the Artist as a Young Man* and *Dubliners*, a collection of short stories.

→ **D.H. Lawrence** Lawrence's novels focus on relationships between men and women, and on the pursuit of individual fulfilment. He grew up in a mining community, and industrialisation often provides a threatening backdrop to his novels. His works include *The Rainbow* and *Women In Love*.

→ **Graham Greene** Greene's heroes are often morally flawed, wrestling with feelings of guilt and desire. Catholicism is an important element in many of his novels, which include *The Power and the Glory*, *The Heart of the Matter* and *Brighton Rock*.

Exam preparation

Find out when the prose fiction text you are studying was first published. (You may already know this; if not, you should be able to find the date at the beginning of the book.) What other prose fiction was published around this time? How is the text typical (or untypical) of the period? How was it received when it was first published?

Take note

One type of experimentation, **magic realism**, was especially influential in the 1970s and 1980s. Magic realism blends realistic representations of life with the improbable and fantastic, often drawing on fairy tale and myth. Authors associated with this approach include **Salman Rushdie** and **Angela Carter**.

Take note

Other significant 20th-century English novelists include: **Virginia Woolf**, **George Orwell**, **Evelyn Waugh**, **Kingsley Amis**, **William Golding**, **Martin Amis**. There have also been important American and Canadian novelists, such as **Margaret Atwood**, **F. Scott Fitzgerald**, **J.D. Salinger**, **Joseph Heller** and **Saul Bellow**. Noted African and Caribbean writers include **V.S. Naipaul** and **Chinua Achebe**.

Take note

Useful sources for the Exam preparation exercise might include:
→ The introduction, notes etc. in your edition of the text.
→ Biographies of the author.
→ English Literature reference books.

Plot and setting

This section looks at the importance in novels and short stories of the main storyline (or **plot**) and of the writer's use of locations and **settings**. Remember that in an exam answer you should never fall into the trap of simply 'telling the story' (examiners sometimes call this **narrative paraphrase**). You should only refer to details of the plot in order to support points about characters, themes, intended effects on the reader and so on.

Plot and structure

The term **plot** refers to the events of a novel and how these are *organised* by the novelist. The pattern or plan that the author imposes on the action of the novel reflects the author's underlying purposes – for example, a sequence of events may be devised that encourages us to be sympathetic towards a character.

The structure of a novel can also be influenced by the novel's form or **genre**. **Epistolary** novels (popular in the 18th century) tell the story through letters written by the main characters. Other novels may take the form of a diary, or have **multiple narrators**, so that events are described from different characters' perspectives. Usually narratives are **linear**, which means events are presented in a chronological sequence, but this is not always the case. For example, there may be **flashbacks**.

When you are considering plot, think about how the overall organisation of the novel, and particular events or sequences of events, illustrate important themes in the novel, or help to convey aspects of the novel's characters. Think also about the kinds of effects the development of the plot has on the reader – for example, parts of the plot may generate a feeling of **suspense**, or the story may have an exciting **climax**.

Setting and themes

The **settings** or locations in a novel, and the ways they are described, can have a range of purposes. Often they reflect the **themes** of the novel in some way. A setting may have a **symbolic** purpose, which means it is used to **represent** something – usually, a set of ideas, attitudes or values. In *Wuthering Heights*, the two main settings are Wuthering Heights itself (a farmhouse on the Yorkshire moors) and another house nearby, Thrushcross Grange. The houses represent contrasting values and approaches to life. Wuthering Heights, a working farm, is associated with the forces of nature and with intense, unrestrained emotion. Thrushcross Grange, a luxurious family residence, is associated with social refinement and control of the emotions. The location of the houses reflects this contrast: Wuthering Heights is set in wild and unprotected moorland ('wuthering' means exposed to violent winds), whereas Thrushcross Grange is set in a sheltered park.

Take note

Examples of novel genres include science fiction, detective novels, gothic novels and historical novels.

Example

Time's Arrow is an experimental novel by Martin Amis which tells the story of a man's life backwards in time, beginning with his death and ending with his childhood.

Take note

As this example illustrates, **contrasts** between settings in a novel can be important.

The jargon

Pathetic fallacy occurs when natural elements (such as landscape or the weather) are used to reflect human moods and emotions. When Heathcliff runs away from Wuthering Heights, fracturing his relationship with Catherine, a violent storm splits a tree in two.

Setting and character

Settings can also be used to reflect aspects of the novel's **characters**. In the case of *Wuthering Heights*, the characters who live at Wuthering Heights tend to be strong and passionate, while those at Thrushcross Grange are delicate and sensitive. In *A Painful Case*, a short story in James Joyce's *Dubliners*, the central character (Mr Duffy) is a morose, emotionally repressed man who avoids human company. His character is reflected in his bleak surroundings and sparsely furnished room:

> He lived in an old sombre house and from his windows he could look into the disused distillery or upwards along the shallow river on which Dublin is built. The lofty walls of his uncarpeted room were free from pictures. He had himself bought every article of furniture in the room: a black iron bedstead, an iron washstand, four cane chairs, a clothes-rack, a coal-scuttle, a fender and irons and a square table on which lay a double desk.

Setting and atmosphere

The **mood** or **atmosphere** evoked by an author's description of a setting can also be important. *The Fall of the House of Usher* is a 19th-century horror story, written by Edgar Allan Poe. The opening sentence, which describes the narrator's journey to the House of Usher, immediately creates an ominous, unsettling atmosphere:

> During the whole of a dull, dark and soundless day in the autumn of the year, when the clouds hung oppressively low in the heavens, I had been passing alone, on horseback, through a singularly dreary tract of country; and at length found myself, as the shades of evening drew on, within view of the melancholy House of Usher.

Short stories

As explained on page 73, most of the material in this chapter is relevant to **short stories** as well as novels. The Poe and Joyce extracts above illustrate this. In the case of **plot**, that of a short story is obviously usually less complex than that of a novel. In fact, short stories often focus on a single revealing incident in the life of a single character. When analysing a story such as this, look for how the central incident is used to explore the character, and how the character changes or develops in the story.

Checkpoint 1

Write a short analysis of this extract, considering how Joyce uses language (especially lexis) to evoke the atmosphere of Mr Duffy's home.

Checkpoint 2

How does the author's use of **pre-modifiers** contribute to the effectiveness of this extract?

Examiner's secrets

If you are studying a collection of short stories, look for similarities and contrasts between the stories. Make a list of the main themes running through the stories, and of the distinctive ways in which the writer uses language.

Exam preparation

See page 85 for a practice question relevant to this section and the section on *Lexis and imagery*.

soot-covered buildings, the continually smoking chimneys, the black canal and the purple river. The ceaseless, repetitive movement of the piston, the sameness of the streets and the endless routine of the people's lives suggest a dreary way of life. The imagery is aural as well as visual: the noise of the factories is suggested by *rattling* and *trembling*. There are unusual comparisons, involving the use of metaphor (*interminable serpents of smoke*) and simile (the brickwork *like the painted face of a savage*, the piston moving *like the head of an elephant in a state of melancholy madness*). Together these images create an atmosphere that is sinister and disturbing. The negative connotations of several words convey the ugliness of the town and the miserable existence of its inhabitants: *vast piles of building, unnatural, monotonously, melancholy*. Repetition (*for ever and ever*) evokes a way of life that never changes. This technique is especially evident in the last sentence, which also uses parallelism, syndetic listing and sentence length to emphasise the repetitive cycle of the inhabitants' lives.

Grammar and phonology

Checkpoints

1 The sentence uses parallelism to emphasise the numerous ways the character has suffered.
2 See page 12 for an explanation of these terms.

Exam preparation

Twain creates the narrative voice of an uneducated American boy. The text has a conversational tone and it is as if Huck is speaking naturally to the reader, who is addressed directly using the second person (*You don't know about me*). The lexis includes colloquial expressions such as *lit out, a body, winds up* and *stretched/stretchers* (meaning exaggeration, or stretching the truth). There is also non-standard spelling, to suggest Huck's unfamiliarity with the word 'civilize' (which becomes *sivilize*). Much of the grammar is non-standard, including double negatives (*I couldn't stand it no longer*), incorrect use of singular and plural verb forms (*There was things*), and non-standard past tense forms (*I never seen*). There are also grammatical constructions that would not appear in standard written English but which suggest the character's speaking voice: *But Tom Sawyer he hunted me up, without you have read*.

Analysing prose fiction extracts

Checkpoints

1 A first-person narrator refers to *I* and *me*. A third-person narrator is not a participant in the story and uses third-person pronouns such as *he*, *she* and *they*.
2 This is grammar that does not conform to the grammatical rules of Standard English.

Revision checklist
Prose fiction

1	Outline the main phases in the development of the English novel.	Confident	Not confident. **Revise** pages 74–75
2	Name the main authors associated with these periods.	Confident	Not confident. **Revise** pages 74–75
3	Explain how the setting of a novel might be significant in relation to themes, characters and atmosphere.	Confident	Not confident. **Revise** pages 76–77
4	Explain the difference between first-person and third-person narration.	Confident	Not confident. **Revise** pages 78–79
5	Understand the term narrative voice.	Confident	Not confident. **Revise** page 78
6	Understand the term unreliable narrator.	Confident	Not confident. **Revise** page 79
7	List the main ways of presenting a character in a novel.	Confident	Not confident. **Revise** pages 80–81
8	Understand how to approach the analysis of a character.	Confident	Not confident. **Revise** page 81
9	Identify the main themes in the prose fiction work you are studying.	Confident	Not confident. **Revise** page 81
10	Explain how fictional dialogue differs from genuine spontaneous speech.	Confident	Not confident. **Revise** page 82
11	List the main functions of dialogue in fiction.	Confident	Not confident. **Revise** page 82
12	Recognise the main forms of fictional dialogue, such as direct and indirect speech.	Confident	Not confident. **Revise** pages 82–83
13	Recognise how levels of formality can differ in prose fiction.	Confident	Not confident. **Revise** page 84
14	Understand the significance of connotations.	Confident	Not confident. **Revise** page 85
15	Comment on the effects achieved by different kinds of sentences in prose fiction.	Confident	Not confident. **Revise** page 86
16	Comment on the effects achieved by non-standard grammar.	Confident	Not confident. **Revise** page 87
17	Approach with confidence the analysis of a prose fiction extract.	Confident	Not confident. **Revise** pages 88–89

Drama

The study of plays is included in all the exam board specifications. With several specifications, there is a particular emphasis on the way spoken language is presented in drama, so the use of **dialogue** to reveal characters, relationships and themes is especially significant. When writing about dramatic texts, you should also try to show that you are aware the text was written to be performed on stage. The set, movements and actions by the characters, and the likely reactions of a live audience are all important elements to consider. You may be studying a contemporary play, or one from the past. If you are studying a Shakespeare play, there is a separate chapter on Shakespeare on pages 115–138.

Exam themes

→ Dramatic form and structure.

→ Dialogue in plays.

→ Characters and themes.

→ Performance elements.

Topic checklist

○ AS ● A2	OCR	EDEXCEL	AQA A	AQA B	WJEC
Historical overview	●	○●	●	●	●
The structure of plays	●	○●	●	●	●
Key features of drama 1	●	○●	●	●	●
Key features of drama 2	●	○●	●	●	●
Dialogue in plays 1	●	○●	●	●	●
Dialogue in plays 2	●	○●	●	●	●
Characters and themes	●	○●	●	●	●
Specimen texts	●	○●	●	●	●

Historical overview

This introductory section gives a brief overview of the history of English drama. The earliest plays set for study at AS and A2 are usually from the Elizabethan and Jacobean period.

Elizabethan and Jacobean drama

Plays of this period were written during the reigns of Elizabeth I (1558–1603) and James I (1603–1625). England's first theatre was built in 1576, and interest in drama escalated in the years that followed. Many famous dramatists belong to this period, which is regarded as the golden age of English drama. **Shakespeare** was the most notable of these dramatists, and his works are discussed in the next chapter (pages 115–138), which also has sections on the historical, social and literary contexts of his plays. Other dramatists of this period include **Christopher Marlowe**, **Ben Jonson** and **John Webster**. Their plays offer penetrating insights into society and the human condition, addressing issues of morality, justice, political discord and social corruption, as well as individual human tragedy. Ben Jonson was a comic **satirist**. In *The Alchemist* he exposes the greed and corruption of a society where people live by material rather than spiritual values.

Restoration comedy

The next important phase in the history of English drama was after the restoration of Charles II in 1660. (In the period immediately preceding this, Charles I had been executed and the Puritans had ordered theatres to be closed.) Restoration comedy was mainly concerned with marriage, sexual desire and infidelity. In many of the plays gullible husbands are duped by their wives and the clever young men they fall in love with. The plays are **comedies of manners**, highlighting the absurdity of much social behaviour. A celebrated example is **William Congreve's** *The Way of the World*. In the 18th century English drama was still mostly comic, though there was less emphasis on sexual intrigue. **Oliver Goldsmith's** *She Stoops to Conquer* (1773) entertainingly ridicules social pretension and general human foolishness.

19th-century drama

The most important 19th-century dramatists emerged towards the end of the century. In particular, the Norwegian playwright **Henrik Ibsen** is generally regarded as the founder of modern drama. His plays broke new ground by addressing contemporary social and political issues. In *A Doll's House*, for example, he examined the social position of married women, portraying a wife who at the end of the play makes the courageous decision to leave her husband. Ibsen is also associated with **naturalism**, a literary movement of the late 19th century which believed in the realistic portrayal of everyday life in novels and plays. Ibsen was an important influence on **George Bernard Shaw**, an Irish-born playwright who lived and worked for most of his life in England. Shaw's first play was produced in 1892, and he continued writing well into the

---

Take note

The earliest English plays date from the Middle Ages. They were performed in the open air by bands of travelling players, on wagons as theatres did not yet exist. The **mystery plays** enacted episodes from the Bible. They were a form of religious instruction, but were also intended to entertain, and included comic scenes and dialogue that incorporated the colloquial language of the time. **Morality plays** developed later, in the late 15th and early 16th centuries. The most admired English example is *Everyman*. The plays use **allegory** to deliver moral lessons. Many morality plays feature the **Vice**, a comic character who is nevertheless the personification of evil. Shakespeare and other later playwrights drew on the traditions of the morality plays, and villains such as Iago in *Othello* have Vice-like characteristics.

The jargon

Comedy of manners is a genre associated with the Restoration and the 18th century. Plays of this kind use clever verbal comedy to examine the attitudes and morals of high society.

Checkpoint 1

Can you explain the difference between **naturalistic** and **stylised** dialogue?

20th century. **Oscar Wilde** was another Irish playwright. His works, such as *The Importance of Being Earnest* (1895), are lighter than those of Ibsen and Shaw but their incisive wit is the vehicle for telling social observation.

Modern drama ●●●

The main trend in modern drama has been the rejection of conventional attitudes and beliefs, mirrored in the abandonment of traditional dramatic forms and conventions.

A key figure in the first half of the 20th century was the German dramatist **Bertolt Brecht**. A typical Brecht play has a series of loosely connected scenes, with songs accompanying the action. Brecht rejected the idea that plays should seek to imitate real life, though his works, such as *Mother Courage* (1941), are strongly political.

The Theatre of the Absurd (discussed more fully on pages 98–99) was a movement that emerged in the 1950s. It sought to reflect the absurdity of existence in plays that deliberately confounded audience expectations of a recognisable plot and coherent dialogue. Playwrights associated with this movement, or influenced by it, include **Samuel Beckett** and **Harold Pinter**.

In contrast, the emphasis in British **kitchen sink drama** of the 1950s was domestic realism. Reacting against the drawing-room comedies and middle-class drama of postwar English theatre, dramatists such as **John Osborne** and **Arnold Wesker** focused on the lives of working- and lower-middle-class characters.

Later British drama has continued to address contemporary issues, though from a variety of perspectives. Brian Friel's *Translations* (1980) is partly a historical drama, examining the effects of English rule in Ireland in the mid-19th century, but the play also has clear relevance to the political situation in Northern Ireland in the closing decades of the 20th century. **Feminist theatre** is another development of the late 20th century. Plays by writers such as **Caryl Churchill** (author of *Top Girls*) and **Pam Gems** celebrate women and challenge the values of patriarchal society.

Checkpoint 2

Can you name any plays written by **George Bernard Shaw**?

Take note

The 20th century also saw the rise of **American** drama, which previously had been of little significance. Writers including **Arthur Miller**, **Tennessee Williams** and **David Mamet** found a large international audience for their plays, though the isues they explore are often of particular relevance to American society. Miller's *Death of a Salesman* (1949) concerns the failure of the American dream. *A Streetcar Named Desire* (1947) by Williams reflects the profound social changes occurring in postwar America. Mamet's *Oleanna* (1992) was a controversial response to the vigorous pursuit of political correctness in American universities.

Take note

Although the texts set for AS and A2 study are usually stage plays, it should be noted that most drama is now written for television and film. Like film, television drama encompasses a range of genres, including soap operas, detective dramas and situation comedies. Another distinction is between series and single plays. Early television plays were shot in a studio, but from the 1960s onwards much television drama has been more cinematic. Important writers include **Jeremy Sandford** (who wrote *Cathy Come Home*, a play about homelessness), **Jimmy McGovern** and **Paul Abbott**.

Exam preparation

Carry out a research investigation into the background of the play you are studying, writing up your findings. When was it written and first performed? What other plays were performed around this time? Are there ways in which the play is typical (or notably untypical) of its period? What other plays did the author write? How does this play compare with these other works – how is it similar, and how different?

Examiner's secrets

Useful sources of information might include: the introduction, notes etc. in the edition you are studying; other editions of the play; literature reference books; Internet sources.

Owen: Cnoc na Ri.

Lancey: If by then the lieutenant hasn't been found, we will proceed
          until a complete clearance is made of this entire section.

Owen: If Yolland hasn't been got by then, they will ravish the whole
          parish.

Lancey: I trust they know exactly what they've got to do.

Text B

Helmer (*from his study*): Is that my little skylark twittering out there?

Nora (*busy opening the parcels*): It is.

Helmer: Scampering about like a little squirrel?

Nora: Yes.

Helmer: When did the squirrel get home?

Nora: Just this minute. (*She slips the bag of macaroons in her pocket
              and wipes her mouth.*) Come in here, Torvald, and you can
              see what I've bought.

Helmer: I'm busy! (*A moment later he opens the door and looks out,
              pen in hand.*) Did you say 'bought'? What, all that? Has my
              little featherbrain been out wasting money again?

Nora: But, Torvald, surely this year we can let ourselves go just a little
              bit? It's the first Christmas that we haven't had to economize.

Helmer: Still, we mustn't waste money, you know.

Nora: Oh, Torvald, surely we can waste a little now – just the
              teeniest bit? Now that you're going to earn a big salary, you'll
              have lots and lots of money.

Helmer: After New Year's Day, yes – but there'll be a whole quarter
              before I get paid.

Nora: Pooh, we can always borrow till then.

Helmer: Nora! (*He goes to her and takes her playfully by the ear.*) The
              same little scatterbrain. Just suppose I borrowed a thousand
              kroner today and you went and spent it all by Christmas, and
              then on New Year's Eve a tile fell on my head, and there I lay –

Nora (*putting a hand over his mouth*): Sh! Don't say such horrid things!

Helmer: But suppose something of the sort were to happen . . .

Nora: If anything as horrid as that were to happen, I don't expect I
              should care whether I owed money or not.

Helmer: But what about the people I'd borrowed from?

Nora: Them? Who bothers about them? They're just strangers.

Helmer: Nora, Nora! Just like a woman! But seriously, Nora, you know
              what I think about that sort of thing. No debts, no borrowing.
              There's something constrained, something ugly even, about a
              home that's founded on borrowing and debt. You and I have
              managed to keep clear up till now, and we shall still do so for
              the little time that is left.

Nora (*going over to the stove*): Very well, Torvald, if you say so.

Helmer (*following her*): Now, now, my little song-bird mustn't be so
              crestfallen. Well? Is the squirrel sulking? (*Taking out his
              wallet*) Nora . . . guess what I have here!

Nora (*turning quickly*): Money!

Helmer: There! (*He hands her some notes.*) Good heavens, I know what
              a lot has to go on housekeeping at Christmas time.

Take note

The question for this text is on page 107.
Torvald is Helmer's first name.

Answers
Drama

Historical overview

Checkpoints

1 These terms are explained on page 106.
2 Shaw's plays include *Saint Joan*, *Pygmalion*, *Arms and the Man*, *Man and Superman*.

The structure of plays

Checkpoints

1 An exposition is a comprehensive explanation or description of something. A resolution is a solution to a problem or dispute.
2 The storylines of comedy dramas such as these are often inconsequential. Nothing much appears to 'happen'.

Key features of drama 1

Checkpoints

1 Properties.
2 To prefigure is to anticipate or look forward to.

Exam preparation

The description of the set establishes the material poverty of Baile Beag (the town in 19th-century Ireland where the play is set). As the play develops, we see the contrast between this poverty and the characters' rich cultural heritage. The set also establishes that it is a rural community, but there is a strong sense of decay and neglect: *a disused barn, broken and forgotten implements*. This is significant because Baile Beag is presented as a society stuck in the past, while the world around it changes. Hugh, the schoolmaster, lives alone at the hedge-school with his son Manus, and their difficult relationship is important in the play. Hugh's wife died some years previously, and this is also reflected in the appearance of the room: it is *comfortless and dusty and functional – there is no trace of a woman's hand*.

Key features of drama 2

Checkpoints

1 *Aural* means related to the sense of hearing.
2 Symbolism occurs when something is used to represent something else. For example, Mitch turning on a light in *A Streetcar Named Desire* represents an attempt to reveal and discover the truth.

Dialogue in plays 1

Checkpoints

1 An unvoiced pause is silent. A filled pause is a sound such as *er* or *um*.
2 Ellipsis.

Exam preparation

Lancey is presented as cold and ruthless as he announces his ultimatum and the brutal punishments that will follow if Yolland is not found. The audience would find these shocking. Lancey's manner is brisk and formal, shown by vocabulary such as *suffice*, *address* and *abode*, and by his use of short, direct sentences (*Lieutenant Yolland is missing. We are searching for him.*). He has an attitude of superiority towards Owen, ignoring his opening question, interrupting his second utterance, addressing him by his surname (*O'Donnell*) and using imperatives to give him instructions (*Do your job. Translate.*). His position on the stage is also significant: when he enters, he takes up a commanding position in the centre of the room. Owen translates Lancey's words as asked, but his shock and disapproval are evident in his reactions. He *stares* at Lancey and at one point begins to protest (*You're not – !*). His translation simplifies Lancey's announcement and makes it less formal. For example, Lancey's *we will shoot all livestock in Ballybeg* becomes *they'll kill every animal in Baile Beag*. However, he also uses more emotive language than Lancey, underlining the horror of what is proposed: *we will proceed until a complete clearance is made of this entire section* becomes *they will ravish the whole parish*. (There is a strong contrast with the earlier translation episode in the play. Then Owen, who was collaborating with the English soldiers, softened Lancey's language, making the proposed survey of the area seem less sinister and threatening.) The recitation of Anglicized versions of Gaelic place names, alternating with their Gaelic equivalents, crystallises the political, cultural and linguistic conflicts in the play and the threat to Irish identity that the English military machine represents.

Dialogue in plays 2

Checkpoints

1 The speech has a logical structure not usually found in natural speech. The first sentence puts forward a proposition, which is then clarified and justified in the two sentences that follow. The second and third sentences neatly balance each other.
2 The pupils ask Briggs questions, looking for information and guidance from him. Briggs also asks questions, but he already knows the answers to them. The forms of address also reflect the differences in status between the characters: the pupils address Briggs as *sir*, but Briggs addresses Ronson by his surname.
3 Examples include *equanimity* and *momentary separation*.
4 Ronson is shown to be sensitive, thoughtful and perceptive.

Exam preparation

The relationship is unequal, and Helmer clearly dominates his wife. At first he is unwilling to speak to Nora, responding to her request that he leave his study by saying, *I'm busy*. He uses patronising address forms when speaking to her: *my little skylark, little squirrel, my little song-bird*. The use of the possessive pronoun *my* indicates Helmer's attitude of ownership and control, and the diminutive adjective *little* emphasises his feeling of superiority. The animal images suggest he regards Nora almost as a domestic pet. His criticisms of her show he doesn't credit her with any intelligence: *featherbrain, scatterbrain*. The period of the play, and the patriarchal society in which it is set, are reflected in the chauvinistic comment *Just like a woman!* He sets rules they must follow as a couple (*No debts, no borrowing*). He teases Nora as if she were a child, only giving her money after asking, *guess what I have here?* At this stage in the play (she acts very differently later), Nora accepts Helmer's authority. She briefly argues that they should borrow money, but soon accepts his decision: *Very well, Torvald, if you say so*. Her acceptance of a subordinate position is also shown by her pleading tone (*surely we can waste a little now*) and by her simple, childlike language: *the teeniest bit, lots and lots of money, a big salary*.

Characters and themes

Checkpoints

1 A dialect is a form of language associated with a group of people (often the inhabitants of a particular geographical region).

2 Estuary English is a version of the London accent, initially associated with an area around the Thames estuary. Research suggests it has steadily spread to other parts of the country.

Revision checklist
Drama

1	Outline the main phases in the development of English drama.	Confident	Not confident. **Revise** pages 96–97
2	Name the main dramatists associated with these periods.	Confident	Not confident. **Revise** pages 96–97
3	Understand the terms exposition, complication, resolution and denouement.	Confident	Not confident. **Revise** page 98
4	Explain the difference between plot and subplot.	Confident	Not confident. **Revise** page 99
5	Understand the ways in which the set of a play might be significant.	Confident	Not confident. **Revise** page 100
6	Understand why a playwright's stage directions are important.	Confident	Not confident. **Revise** page 101
7	Recognise the significance of performance elements, including costume, lighting, music and sound effects.	Confident	Not confident. **Revise** pages 102–103
8	Explain the term dramatic irony.	Confident	Not confident. **Revise** page 103
9	Explain how dramatic dialogue differs from real speech.	Confident	Not confident. **Revise** page 104
10	Identify the main purposes of dramatic dialogue.	Confident	Not confident. **Revise** page 105
11	Understand the differences between stylised and naturalistic dialogue.	Confident	Not confident. **Revise** pages 106–107
12	Approach with confidence the analysis of dramatic dialogue.	Confident	Not confident. **Revise** page 107
13	Understand the terms hero, protagonist and antagonist.	Confident	Not confident. **Revise** page 108
14	List the main ways of presenting a character in a play.	Confident	Not confident. **Revise** page 108
15	Identify the ways in which a character might be important to the play as a whole.	Confident	Not confident. **Revise** page 109
16	Identify the main themes in the play you are studying.	Confident	Not confident. **Revise** page 109

Shakespeare

Plays by Shakespeare feature on all the exam board specifications, though they are optional on some specifications and compulsory on others. Usually questions require both close analysis of an extract and the discussion of a broader aspect of the play as a whole. The main focus in this chapter is on the distinctive characteristics of Shakespeare's language, and on the strategies you should adopt when examining a Shakespeare extract. The early sections of the chapter give an overview of Shakespeare's plays, and the chapter also includes a section on Shakespeare in performance. You should always remember that Shakespeare wrote his plays to be performed on stage, and if you have the opportunity you should certainly try to see a production of the play you are studying. If that is not possible, an alternative is to watch a video or DVD version.

Exam themes

→ Shakespeare's language.

→ Dialogue in Shakespeare's plays.

→ Context of Shakespeare's plays.

→ Performance elements.

Topic checklist

O AS ● A2	OCR	EDEXCEL	AQA A	AQA B	WJEC
Shakespeare: an overview	●	O	●	●	●
Shakespeare in context	●	O	●	●	●
Shakespeare's language 1	●	O	●	●	●
Shakespeare's language 2	●	O	●	●	●
Shakespeare's language 3	●	O	●	●	●
Dialogue in Shakespeare	●	O	●	●	●
Analysing Shakespeare extracts 1	●	O	●	●	●
Analysing Shakespeare extracts 2	●	O	●	●	●
Shakespeare in performance	●	O	●	●	●
Specimen texts	●	O	●	●	●

Lexis

→ How does the vocabulary that is used reflect the personalities of individual **characters**, and the way they are feeling at this particular point in the play? In *Othello*, for instance, there is a contrast between the grand, elevated diction of Othello and the blunt, coarse language often associated with Iago.

→ What **imagery** (similes/metaphors) is present? What effect does it have? Are there links between any of the images that are present and the imagery found elsewhere in the play?

→ What about the effects achieved by **individual words**? What connotations do these words have? Are they shocking, evocative, revealing, powerful?

→ Are any **key words** present – words that are important because they occur repeatedly in the play as a whole (e.g. the word *honest* in *Othello*)?

→ Are any **rhetorical** devices used, such as repetition, antithesis, wordplay and hyperbole?

→ Is there any **dramatic irony**? Is anything said that has an extra significance, which the character speaking the words is unaware of?

→ How do the characters **address** each other? Are these modes of address significant or revealing?

→ Does the lexis in any way **echo** vocabulary found somewhere else in the play? Or are there **contrasts**?

Grammar

→ What **types of sentence** are used? Declarative, imperative, interrogative, exclamatory? How does this reflect the moods or attitudes of the speakers at particular points in the extract?

→ How **long** are the sentences? Are any especially long, or especially short? If so, what effect does this have?

→ Are any effects achieved by **word order**? Are any particular words or phrases foregrounded (made to stand out), for example by placing them at the beginning or end of lines and sentences?

→ Is there any kind of **rhetorical** patterning in the way sentences are organised – for example, parallelism?

→ How do any of these grammatical elements reflect **themes** of the play, or aspects of the **characters** who are speaking? In *The Tempest*, for instance, Prospero is a figure of authority and as a result often uses imperative sentences.

Links

See pages 122–123 for more on the rhetorical devices found in Shakespeare.

Checkpoint 1

Words and phrases can also be foregrounded by **inverted syntax**. What is inverted syntax?

Checkpoint 2

Explain the term **parallelism**.

Exam preparation

There are two specimen Shakespeare extract questions at the end of the next section, on page 131.

Analysing Shakespeare extracts 2

This second section on Shakespeare extract questions looks at two other language frameworks (**phonology** and **discourse structure**), at what you might say about the **staging** of an extract, and at other factors to consider when you offer your **interpretation** of the extract.

Phonology

→ Are any **phonological devices** such as alliteration, onomatopoeia, assonance and sibilance used? (Remember you should only mention these if you are confident they have a particular effect, and you can explain what this effect is.)

→ Is **blank verse** used? If so, does the metre cause significant words to be stressed? Is the metre disturbed or altered at any point, and if so why does this happen? If the metre is steady and regular, why might this be appropriate?

→ How would **intonation** influence the effect that the extract has? With what tone of voice should particular words or lines be delivered? Are there lines that could be said in different ways? In *The Winter's Tale*, when Hermione succeeds in persuading Polixenes to stay in Sicilia, her husband Leontes comments, *At my request he would not*. Depending on how it is delivered, this could appear a straightforward observation or a line suggesting deep suspicion.

→ Is **pace** significant at any point? Are particular lines said especially quickly or slowly? Are there any changes in pace?

→ If the extract were heard in performance, what part would **volume** play? Would some lines be shouted, or said especially quietly?

Discourse structure

→ Is the extract a passage of **dialogue**, a single **speech** by a character (with other characters present), or a **soliloquy** (a speech delivered by a character alone on stage)?

→ If it is **dialogue**, how do the characters **interact**? (For more on this, see *Dialogue in Shakespeare*, pages 126–127.

→ If it is a **soliloquy**, what is revealed about the character's innermost thoughts? What kind of relationship does the character have with the audience? Often soliloquies make the audience feel closer to the character concerned.

→ Are there any **asides**? These occur when a character says something the other characters do not hear. They can serve a variety of purposes: characters may share private jokes with the audience, reveal what they are secretly thinking or make candid observations about what is taking place on stage.

→ Is the extract **prose** or **poetry**, or a mixture of the two? You may be able to comment on the likely reason for this (see page 121).

→ How does the extract **start**, **develop** and **end**? Are there any changes of mood or atmosphere? Does the extract build to a climax?

Checkpoint 1

Explain the terms **assonance** and **sibilance**.

Checkpoint 2

What collective term is used for spoken language features such as intonation, pace and volume?

The jargon

Discourse structure refers to the overall form and structure of the extract.

Example

Iago's soliloquies in *Othello* make us aware of his villainous intentions, but we are also likely to admire his wit and his incisive intelligence.

Staging

→ How would the extract be **presented on stage**? Try to visualise it (if you have seen a performance or watched a video of the play, this will obviously help).

→ Are there any **stage directions**? Note that sometimes characters' actions are indicated by what is said rather than by explicit stage directions.

→ Are the characters' **actions** in any way significant? What impact do they have on the audience?

→ Where are the characters **positioned** on stage? What does this tell us?

→ Do **sound effects** (such as music) play a part in the scene?

Interpretation

Here are some additional points you should bear in mind when interpreting the meaning and significance of the extract:

→ Don't just 'tell the story'. You need to **comment** on the characters' words and actions.

→ Focus on how the **language** of the extract develops our understanding of **characters and their relationships**, and of the **themes** in the play.

→ Consider the **dramatic effect** that an extract has. Note that 'dramatic' here doesn't have its everyday sense of exciting and out of the ordinary. It refers to the effects that are achieved when the play is performed in front of an audience.

→ Remember to **make connections with the rest of the play**, especially if the question you are answering specifies that you should do this. Look for similarities and contrasts with other parts of the play, and think about the significance of the extract in relation to what has preceded it and what happens later.

→ Are any aspects of the extract open to **alternative interpretations**? It might be possible (if relevant) to refer to one or more of the **critical approaches** to Shakespeare outlined on page 119.

→ It is important to consider the **context** the extract has within the play as a whole (see page 128). However, it may also be relevant to refer to the play's broader social, political or historical **contexts** (see page 118).

Exam preparation (45 minutes) answer: page 137

Texts C and **D** on page 135 are from *The Tempest* and *Measure for Measure* respectively. Choose one of the extracts and answer the following question on it:
Comment closely on Shakespeare's use of language in this extract. Develop your answer by discussing the significance of the extract in relation to the play as a whole.

Examiner's secrets

The main focus of your answer should usually be on the **language** of the extract, but you will also be given credit if you show you are aware the extract was written to be performed on stage.

Watch out!

Remember that when you are writing about plays you should refer to the *audience* rather than to the *reader*.

Examples

The main dramatic effect of an extract might be to cause amusement, build a sense of anticipation, create an atmosphere of conflict or confusion and so on.

Take note

If you are not studying either of these plays, you could still attempt an analysis of the language of Text C, which is the beginning of *The Tempest*. Develop your answer by commenting on the effectiveness of the extract as an opening to a play.

Shakespeare in performance

Links

See page 119 for more on the theatres of Shakespeare's day.

Although you will rightly spend much of your time reading your Shakespeare text, it is important to remember that Shakespeare's plays were written to be performed on stage. This section considers how the plays were influenced by the performance conventions of Elizabethan and Jacobean theatre, and also how producers and performers today are able to offer contrasting interpretations of individual plays.

The importance of language

As explained on page 119, theatres in Shakespeare's time did not have artificial lighting and also made very little use of scenery or props. In contrast, today's dramatists can if they choose achieve effects through the use of lighting and elaborate stage sets, as well as technological devices such as revolving stages, back-projection and computer-generated images. Because these resources were not available to Elizabethan dramatists, **language** was crucial to the creation of mood, atmosphere and a sense of location.

You should look out for examples of this in the play you are studying. In *The Tempest*, for instance, the island where the play is set is created in our imaginations by the **visual imagery** of passages such as this:

Checkpoint 1

Apart from our sense of sight, what other senses does this description appeal to? What are these kinds of image known as?

> So I charmed their ears,
> That, calf-like, they my lowing followed, through
> Toothed briers, sharp furzes, pricking goss, and thorns,
> Which entered their frail shins. At last I left them
> I' th' filthy-mantled pool beyond your cell,
> There dancing up to th'chins, that the foul lake
> O'erstunk their feet.

Visual and aural effects

Examiner's secrets

Although in writing about Shakespeare your primary focus will usually be on the language of the plays, you will also be given credit if you show an awareness of effects that are dependent on the play being seen in performance.

Although Elizabethan theatres made limited use of scenery, visual effects could still be achieved by the characters' **costumes** and by their **actions**. Shakespeare's plays are often enlivened by dynamic events such as swordfights, battle-scenes, dances and processions. Sometimes actions are understated but still powerful, as in the chilling moment when Othello and Iago kneel together and commit themselves to vengeance on Desdemona and Cassio. The main sound effect was the use of **music** (again *The Tempest*, where music helps to create the island's magical atmosphere, is a good example of this).

Dramatic conventions

Some other dramatic conventions of Shakespeare's time are worth noting:

Checkpoint 2

Explain the difference between a **soliloquy** and an **aside**.

→ The use of **soliloquies** and **asides**. The closeness of spectators to the stage meant that characters could share jokes with the audience, and give the impression of confiding in them.

→ The occasional use of **prologues** and **epilogues** to begin and end plays.

→ The use of **blank verse** and **rhetoric** – dialogue was generally not meant to appear realistic (see pages 120 and 122–123).

→ The use of certain stock **character types**, such as the tragic hero, the revenger and the malcontent. Shakespeare drew on tradition and convention here, but still created characters who are individuals rather than stereotypes.

→ The **absence of act or scene divisions**. These did not exist in the versions of Shakespeare's plays printed during his lifetime. The divisions inserted by later editors mark natural breaks in the action, but contemporary productions of Shakespeare's plays would have been faster and more free-flowing than we are used to today.

→ The exclusive use of **male actors**, even for female roles. It is thought that women's parts were usually played by apprentice actors in their early teens (though mature characters such as Lady Macbeth and Cleopatra were probably played by older apprentices).

Performance and interpretation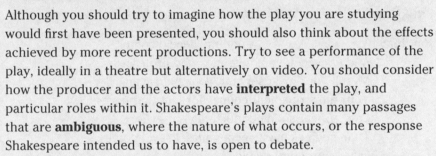

Although you should try to imagine how the play you are studying would first have been presented, you should also think about the effects achieved by more recent productions. Try to see a performance of the play, ideally in a theatre but alternatively on video. You should consider how the producer and the actors have **interpreted** the play, and particular roles within it. Shakespeare's plays contain many passages that are **ambiguous**, where the nature of what occurs, or the response Shakespeare intended us to have, is open to debate.

The closing scene of *Measure for Measure* is an example. The Duke proposes to Isabella, who says nothing and remains silent for the rest of the play. Clearly a wide range of possible non-verbal reactions are available to the actress playing Isabella – should she look pleased, uncomfortable, angry?

More broadly, a producer can aim for specific effects by setting the play in a particular historical period (including the present day) or by emphasising particular aspects of it. Productions of *Othello*, for example, sometimes see the hero as primarily a victim of a racist society, and highlight this by changing the play's setting.

Links

See page 119 for more on how Shakespeare's plays are open to a variety of interpretations.

Exam preparation (45 minutes)

Write an essay on the opening scene of the Shakespeare play you are studying, discussing how the staging of the scene might contribute to its overall effect. You might refer to productions you have seen, or to how you would choose to stage the play yourself.

→ **Journalese** is more common in tabloids. These are newspaper clichés – words that occur repeatedly in newspapers, such as *storm*, *soar*, *row*, *probe*, *boost*.

→ Lexis in tabloids is often more obviously **emotive**, **dramatic** and **sensational**. Modifiers often have an emotional impact (e.g. *tragic*, *brave*). Broadsheets tend to be more factual and informative.

→ **Bias** tends to be more obvious in tabloids. Words often have connotations that are clearly positive or negative. In broadsheets the tone may be more neutral, or bias may be expressed more subtly.

Grammar ●●●

→ Tabloids use a large number of **short sentences**, which are often **simple** or **compound**. In broadsheets sentences tend to be **longer**, making more demands upon the reader. **Complex** sentences, often with two or more subordinate clauses, occur more frequently.

→ **Fronted conjunctions** (which occur when sentences begin with a conjunction such as *And* or *But*) are more common in tabloids.

→ Tabloids often rely on **simple connectives** (especially *and*, *but*, *now*) to achieve **cohesion**. In broadsheets a wider range of cohesive devices is employed.

Discourse structure ●●●

→ The **opening paragraphs** of news reports usually summarise the key facts.

→ In tabloids, **paragraphs** are generally **short** and often only one sentence long. In broadsheets, paragraphs tend to be **longer**, and articles as a whole tend to be more **detailed**.

→ **Closing paragraphs** are often used to provide background information or to give the latest available news.

Graphology ●●●

→ In tabloids there is more extensive use of **graphological features**, to make the text eye-catching and accessible.

→ Tabloids avoid too much **dense text**. Articles are usually short and paragraphs are also brief.

→ In tabloids there is more **typographical variation**, with the use of bold print, italics etc.

Links

Modifiers are explained on page 10.

Links

Cohesion is explained on page 14.

Watch out!

Graphological features are also important in broadsheets, but the use of graphology is more restrained. Written text is more prominent than in tabloids.

Exam preparation (30 minutes)   answer: pages 150–151

Text D on page 149 is an editorial from the *Daily Mirror*. **Text E** is part of an editorial from *The Observer*. Compare the use of language in these texts.

Take note

On page 149 there is also information on the background to these two editorials.

New technology texts

The AS/A2 specifications require you to study texts of different types and from different periods, so you should be familiar with the language features of the new types of text that are emerging as a result of developments in technology. This section looks at three examples: **websites**, **e-mail** and **text messages**.

Websites

Some websites only differ from traditional written texts in that printed material is presented on a screen rather than on a page, but others have features that make websites a distinctive form of text:

→ The way material is **organised** and **presented** is influenced by the dimensions of the screen. Text that runs along the top or bottom of the screen, or down the margins, is common.

→ Much of the text is **non-linear**. Traditional linear text is read progressively from the top of the page to the bottom, but on websites separate sections of text occupy different parts of the screen, and we do not read them in a fixed sequence (there is some similarity here with a page in a newspaper). There may be a main body of text, but additional material, such as advertisements and links to other pages or sites, is also usually present.

→ Partly because of the size of the screen, information is **broken down** into manageable segments. Headings, lists and summaries are common, and paragraphs are generally short.

→ **Graphological features** are important, with the use of colour, animation and visual images. In written text colour coding or underlining may be used to indicate hypertext links.

→ Websites are much more **interactive** than traditional written texts. If you are buying goods or booking a flight, for example, you will be asked to provide information in a set sequence. More proactively, you might choose to enlarge or transfer visual images from a site.

E-mail

As with websites, not all e-mails differ significantly from their traditional written equivalents: some are very similar to letters. However, it is also the case that many e-mails do have distinctive linguistic characteristics. In particular, the **informality** of e-mail, together with the **interactive** relationship between senders and receivers (especially evident in Internet chatrooms), makes it a form of written communication that is in many ways close to **spoken** language. Significant features of e-mail language include:

→ **Lexis** is often **conversational**, with the frequent use of colloquialisms and contractions. There is more tolerance of **spelling errors** than in traditional texts: messages are typed out quickly, and are not usually checked for errors (some non-standard spelling may be deliberate – see below).

Checkpoint 1

Can you think of any other genres that feature **non-linear** text?

Take note

New technology has created a huge number of **neologisms** (new words and expressions), sometimes known collectively as **cyberspeak** or **netspeak**. Here are just a few examples:

→ **WAP** An acronym from 'wireless application protocol', referring to technology that enables mobile phones and other radio devices to be connected to the Internet.

→ **ISP** An initialism, short for 'Internet Service Provider'.

→ **Clickthrough** The number of visitors to a site.

→ **Silver surfer** A retired person who uses the Internet frequently.

→ **Yettie** A young person who makes money from the Internet (an acronym derived from 'young entrepreneurial technocrat').

Checkpoint 2

What are **contractions**?

→ **Greetings** and **farewells** illustrate the informality of the medium. *Hi* has become a standard way of opening messages, though sometimes greetings are dispensed with altogether as the names of sender and receiver automatically appear at the top of the message.

→ **Grammatical features** include **loosely constructed sentences**, which resemble the natural flow of speech. In order to type messages more quickly, some **punctuation marks** may be omitted, and **lower case letters** used where standard grammar would usually require capitals.

→ Various methods are used to suggest the **prosodic features** of speech, such as stress and tone of voice. These include upper case letters to indicate emphasis, non-standard spelling to suggest pronunciation and multiple punctuation marks (especially exclamation marks) to convey intonation:

> I was SOOooo PLEASED to see you last night!!!

→ A large number of **abbreviations** are used in e-mails, Internet chatrooms and mobile phone text messages. Examples include *BBL* ('be back later'), *MYOB* ('mind your own business') and *JK* ('just kidding').

→ **Emoticons** (also known as **smileys**) are graphical symbols used to represent facial expressions and body language:

> :-) smile
> :-(anger, displeasure
> {} a hug

Text messages

The main influence on text messaging style is the need to keep messages as short and concise as possible. The small screen size (which usually accommodates about 160 characters) and the small keypad encourage compression, and shorter messages also take less time to compose. In addition to **abbreviations** and **emoticons** (see above), linguistic features found in text messages include:

→ **Words are shortened**, as in *TXT* (for 'text') and *TLK* (for 'talk'). As these examples illustrate, it is often vowels that are dropped.

→ **Phonetic spelling**, as in *LUV* (for 'love') and *NE* (for 'any').

→ **Letter homophones**, as in *C* (for 'see') and *U* (for 'you').

→ **Number homophones**, as in *2* (for 'to') and *4* (for 'for').

→ **Grammatical compression** Determiners, auxiliary verbs etc. are often omitted from sentences, and punctuation marks may also be missing.

Take note

The stylistic features of text messages are not entirely new. Telegrams made use of grammatical compression, and the Phoenicians (one of the first civilisations to develop writing) used an alphabet made up entirely of consonants, with no vowel sounds.

Take note

On Valentines Day in 2003, an estimated 70 million text messages were sent in Britain. This far exceeded the number of Valentine cards received on the same day.

Exam preparation (15 minutes)   answer: page 151

Text C on page 149 is a series of messages from an Internet chatroom.
Comment on the use of language in these messages.

Specimen texts

The texts below are for use with the practice exam questions for this chapter.

Take note

The question for this text is on page 141. Private Horace Bruckshaw fought at Gallipoli during the First World War, and the diary entries are from this period. On a visit home he left the diaries with his wife. Later in the war he fought in France, where he was killed in 1917.

Text A

Sunday, 9 May 1915. Spent a rotten night of it. This is a terrible place simply infested with snipers. Nine of us went out with Capt. Andrews hunting them during the morning. Could find nothing however although we were sniped at every step we took. Luckily we all got safely back to our trench. Chapman wounded in chest this morning just as he got up to go to the assistance of another wounded man. It made us a wee bit nervous as he was sitting against me. After dark we went over the back of the trench to a point about a mile back to fetch rations up. We had just returned when the Turks greeted us with a fusillade of rapid fire. This they kept up all night.

Monday, 10 May. Things went quieter by breakfast time but the snipers kept very busy. We laid pretty low all day. We have lost nearly all our officers with these blessed snipers. Captain Tetley is the latest victim having been hit in both legs while leading a party sniper hunting. Very few of them got back again. Heavy firing commenced at dusk and continued all night.

Take note

The question for this text is on page 143. The complete advertisement features a photograph of a woman in an EasyJet uniform talking to another womam on a train.

Text B

So I'm on this train, right? Wednesday morning. Going to work. I start chatting to this girl sitting opposite me. She saw my uniform and, like a lot of people, started to ask me a few questions about my work. It's usually the same thing they want to know – people always think that you just wear loads of makeup, flirt with pilots and do 'that thing' with your arms before take off! So I set her straight. There's a lot more to working for **easyJet** than that. We're there to make sure every single passenger on every single aircraft has exactly the flight they want. Sometimes they just want to read. Sometimes they just want a reassuring word or smile. And, on occasion, when we've got a group of lads off on a stag do, they'll want a little more than that! The one thing they all have in common is that my fellow Crew and I are responsible for them. And working for **easyJet**, unlike some other airlines, we get more of a chance to be ourselves. And if there's anything orange about us, it's our uniforms, not our make up . . .

To find out more about the role and how to apply for a position at our London Stansted, Gatwick and Luton bases, visit the cabin crew jobs page at www.easyJet.com/en/jobs

Take note

The question for this text is on page 147.

Text C

>>JillyB<JillyB@postchat.co.uk wrote:
>>>how have the holidays been treating everyone?
>>>lots of lounging about I trust.

Jimbo@postchat.co.uk
>>Lounging and some blowing-of-the-gift-money shopping today. And
>>I don't have to be back at work until January 5!

Geoff<Geoff@postchat.co.uk wrote:
>I am doing the very same! I got a new BOOK! Off to read it!
>Jimbo, What day you wanna hang out? Tues, Wed or Thurs? Not free Fri or Sat or Sun!!!

DON'T GIVE SICK KILROY A PLATFORM

For anyone to write about Arabs as Robert Kilroy-Silk did would be damn stupid.

For a well-known BBC presenter to do it was absurd.

Newspaper columnists enjoy being provocative but that is not the same as being downright offensive, insulting and racist.

Ever since the terrible events of 9/11, responsible people throughout the West have tried to explain that not all Arabs are terrorists. It is ridiculous to suggest they are – and to do so displays the same narrow-minded, blinkered view of the world which is the hallmark of fanatics.

Robert Kilroy-Silk had a special responsibility. As the BBC has learnt, its leading presenters are seen as speaking for the Corporation – although they obviously are not – and some countries will even believe that what they say is sanctioned by the BBC or government.

Yet Kilroy-Silk heaped mindless, disgraceful abuse on all Arabs.

Unbelievably, the Sunday Express fully supports him, insisting what he said is not racist, thus confirming that their editor is a complete idiot.

The BBC, though, has rightly suspended Kilroy. He has no place on our screens while he spouts such dangerous, nasty nonsense.

KILROY-SILK IS AN ASS. SO IS THE BBC

effusions on daytime television, there is something deeply disturbing about the BBC's response which has been to shelve Kilroy-Silk's programme pending an investigation. Given that the man has apologised and the circumstances of how the column was mistakenly reprinted are now understood, we wonder what there is to investigate, particularly since the original article was read by millions nine months ago without raising a murmur.

Take note

The question for this text is on page 145. In January 2004 the television presenter Robert Kilroy-Silk was suspended by the BBC after he made controversial comments about Arab countries in an article he wrote for the *Sunday Express*. **Text D** is an editorial from the *Daily Mirror*, giving the newspaper's views on the matter. **Text E** is part of an editorial from *The Observer*.

how aspects of the language you have used are appropriate (e.g. you might say, *I have used complex, polysyllabic vocabulary because the text is aimed at a mature, educated audience*).

Lexis

This includes use of: **informal** vocabulary (e.g. **colloquial** expressions, **contractions**); **formal** vocabulary; **simple** (possibly **monosyllabic**) or **complex** (possibly **polysyllabic**) vocabulary; **semantic fields**; words with **positive** or **negative connotations**; words with specific **connotations**; **emotive** vocabulary; **pre-modifiers** and **post-modifiers**; **repetition** of key words; **similes** and **metaphors**; **visual**, **auditory**, **tactile**, **gustatory** and **olfactory imagery**; **deictic** expressions; **puns** and other kinds of **humour**.

Checkpoint 1

Explain the differences between **visual**, **auditory**, **tactile**, **gustatory** and **olfactory imagery**.

Grammar

Use of: **declarative**, **interrogative**, **imperative** and **exclamatory** sentences; **simple**, **compound** and **complex** sentences; **short** and **long** sentences; **ellipsis**; **parallelism**; **foregrounding**; **syndetic** and **asyndetic** listing; **first**, **second** and **third person**; **past**, **present** and **future tense**.

Checkpoint 2

Explain the difference between a **simple** and a **compound** sentence.

Phonology

Use of: **onomatopoeia**; **alliteration**; **rhyme**; **rhythmic effects**; **stress** and **intonation**; **pauses**; **repetition**; **sound effects**.

Discourse content and structure

Includes discussion of: how you've **started**; how you've **organised** your points (e.g. **order**, use of **paragraphs**); how you've **finished**; what you've **included**, and what you haven't; how you've achieved **cohesion**; in stories, **development** of **plot** and **character**, and balance of **description**, **action** and **dialogue**.

Graphology

Use of **layout** and **visual features**.

Watch out!

Students often write too much on graphology. Be careful not to do this.

Comparative commentaries ●●●

In **comparative commentaries**, you include points such as those listed above, but develop the points further by explaining how your text **compares** with the source texts, commenting in particular on the **differences** and on the **reasons** for any changes you have made. In the commentary it is usually appropriate to **quote** from the source texts as well as from your own text, in order to illustrate the points made.

Exam preparation (40 minutes)   answer: page 167

Write a commentary of approximately 400 words to accompany your answer to the text transformation exercise on page 161.

Specimen texts

The texts below are for use with the practice exam questions on pages 161 and 163.

Take note

Text A is an abridged version of an article by Colin Cottell that appeared in *The Guardian* newspaper on 20 December 2003.

Text A

It ain't what you do, it's the way that you say it

Some people will do whatever it takes to get ahead in their career. Change job, move house, ingratiate themselves with their boss. Even change their accent.

'I want to neutralise my accent,' says Victoria Hardy, an image consultant. She moved to Glasgow after a childhood spent in the north-east. Now Ms Hardy is taking lessons from Derek Rogers, a language and accent specialist from Glasgow.

'I am doing it for career purposes really, to achieve maximum impact when I speak so everyone understands what I am saying,' she says.

You might think that Ms Hardy is paranoid or insecure. But a recent study by the Aziz Corporation, a firm of image consultants, suggests otherwise. It found that 46% of company directors believe that having a strong regional accent is considered a disadvantage to business success.

It also showed that some accents are more unequal than others. Liverpudlian, Brummie, West Country and Cockney accents came out worst. But Home Counties' and Scottish accents are seen as career assets.

The study confirmed previous research, which showed that having the wrong type of accent can affect your career. It also added credence to the belief that the 'acceptability' of local accents is a key factor in companies' decisions about where to locate.

'I think it is blind prejudice,' says Khalid Aziz, chairman of the Aziz Corporation. 'It seems to be pretty general. It is not just that southerners don't like people from the north; traditionally the Scots don't like the English. It works all ways round. The fact is that it is not what you say, but the way that you say it.'

Jenni Hunt, a lawyer from Wimbledon, and originally from Worksop, used to speak with a south Yorkshire accent. But after leaving her home town 16 years ago, she says she ditched her twang. 'I wanted to be taken seriously and to take myself seriously. I am pretty sure that it has helped my career,' she says.

In an attempt to boost her other career performing voiceovers she is having one-to-one sessions with Frances Parkes, a speech coach, and head of www.makethemostofyourvoice.com.

'When I ring up agents I speak with my lawyer's voice, the one I use for meetings,' says Ms Hunt.

People make assumptions about you based on your accent, says Ms Hardy. 'Every accent has a stigma attached to it in various ways. I don't want people to think about my accent. I want them to focus on what I am actually saying.'

Inquiries? Now the accent is on profit

Bin the brogue and adopt a cut-glass Home Counties voice. That was once the best advice for ambitious Celts and northerners. But now, amid the chaos of directory inquiry deregulation, comes victory for regional accents.

Traditional southern English is no match for a Scottish lilt, charming Irish chirp or warm Welsh warble when dealing with irate callers, and most inquiries to the controversial new 118 numbers are being handled by centres in northern England and the Celtic fringe. You may not be told the price of the call, you may not even get the right number, but at least you will be greeted by a dulcet tone.

The dominance of regional accents in call centres may be put down to the establishment of operations in areas where land is cheaper and jobs harder to come by than in the South-East, but telecoms bosses admit that accents played a part in determining where they settled.

Cable and Wireless, the biggest operator of new numbers coming on stream from today, said its research showed callers preferred to be greeted by northern and Scottish accents. It operates its services from three main centres, two of which are in Glasgow.

Philip Cheal of C&W said: 'Some accents are consistently more popular and trusted. The main thing is that calls are taken by someone with a clear voice who speaks politely to the customer. People are not turned down for a job on the grounds of their accent.'

The Number has launched its 118 118 directory service from a call centre in Cardiff and last week announced it had created 2,000 jobs. Its decision to locate in Wales was partly driven by the accent. 'The accents of people living near our call centres do lend themselves to this type of work,' said a spokesman.

The southern accent has also lost ground in broadcasting. Younger presenters including the BBC's Brummie Adrian Chiles, Welshman Huw Edwards and Scotswoman Kirsty Wark have not had to go all Cholmondeley-Warner to get ahead in the game. In recent years there have even been howls from some sectors within the BBC that plummy accents were proving a barrier to promotion.

The BBC has made a conscious move to diversify accents on Radios 3 and 4 in the past decade, admitting it had lagged 'a little behind the sound of the nation – beginning to sound a bit antique.'

However, callers to the new numbers say they are less interested in the telephonists' voices than in their ability to find the right numbers. Sheila MacMillan, 35, a Glasgow teacher, said yesterday: 'I phoned a 118 line for the number of a charity's head office in London. The operator had a pleasant accent but proved useless at finding the number. I ended up speaking to a shop assistant in Bromley. She had a nice accent, too, but it was a waste of 10 minutes and £2.'

Take note

Text B is an abridged version of an article by Stephen Khan that appeared in *The Observer* newspaper on 24 August 2003.

Answers
Writing and adapting texts

Original writing 1

Checkpoints

1 Stories written for young children are one type of text that might have both a reading audience and a listening audience.
2 Other fiction genres include: romantic fiction, historical novels, war stories, ghost stories, epistolary novels (stories told in the form of letters).

Exam preparation

To persuade: Charity appeal; publicity material; radio advertisement script; speech on a controversial issue.

To inform (note that in some cases the primary purpose of the following might be to persuade or to entertain): Newspaper article; magazine feature; sports report; book review; film review; album review; review of a live performance; guide to a local amenity; beginner's guide; autobiographical writing; biographical writing; guide for new students; handbook for new employees; educational text; travel journalism; CD liner notes; health information leaflet; Internet text; radio talk; audio guide script.

To entertain: Short story; beginning of a novel; radio play; film or television script; comedy sketch.

To instruct: Instruction booklet.

Original writing 2

Checkpoints

1 Groups of words with meanings linked to a particular field or topic.
2 These are sometimes known as 'pointing' words. They only make sense if they are related to the immediate situation or context – e.g. *now, yesterday, here, there*.

Adapting and transforming texts 1

Checkpoints

1 .The audience might be addressed more directly (e.g. by the use of interrogatives and of the second person). The text might incorporate phonological/prosodic features.
2 When the text was written might be important. The circumstances in which the text was intended to be read or listened to might also be significant.

Adapting and transforming texts 2

Checkpoints

1 To paraphrase is to express the same meaning in different words.
2 This refers to the various techniques used to link the different parts of a text together. See page 14.

Exam preparation

In tackling this question you initially need to make sure you have a clear understanding of the four GASP elements (genre, audience, subject, purpose). The genre is prepared speech. The fact that you are being asked to produce a *spoken* text has important implications for the kind of language you will need to use. The immediate audience are in the studio, but there is also a wider audience of radio listeners. In both cases they are likely to have an interest in current affairs and to be aged from late teens upwards. The subject is regional accents and whether schools should seek to change them. The purpose is partly to inform the audience about the topic, but mainly to persuade them to share your views.

You should also think about language features that could be included in your answer. These will need to be appropriate to the four GASP elements. For example, lexical features might include: a generally formal register (to reflect the context – a current affairs radio programme); occasional informality (to achieve a rapport with the audience); relevant semantic fields (such as education and regional accents); monosyllabic words (to make clear, direct statements); polysyllabic words (to reflect the seriousness and complexity of the topic); persuasive, positive lexis (used to present views you agree with); negative lexis (used to present views you disagree with); emotive vocabulary (to move and persuade the audience). Possible grammatical features include: declarative sentences (to present your views); use of second person and of interrogative sentences (to address and involve the audience); occasional use of short sentences (to make points clearly and forcefully); rhetorical techniques such as parallelism, repetition, contrast and tripling (to achieve emphasis and rhythmic effects). Phonology will be important as the text is for a listening audience. Use of different types of sentence will help to give the talk varied intonation, and as mentioned rhetorical techniques can be used to achieve a strong sense of rhythm. In the script pauses for effect and stress on particular words might also be indicated. The discourse structure will partly depend on the points you intend to include (see below). You need to think about how to introduce and conclude the talk, and the rest of it needs to have a logical structure.

Two texts are provided as source material. You should read through these carefully, looking for ideas and information you can use. It is important to make use of *both* texts, even if one appeals to you more than the other.

Here is a specimen answer to the question:

If you think you have a good ear for regional accents, you might be surprised to hear that I'm a student at a college in Liverpool. However, if you think you can detect the unmistakable vowel sounds of a north Londoner you'd actually be quite right, because I grew up in Camden Town. I've lived in Liverpool for four years now and I'm pleased to say that in all that time none of my teachers has made any attempt to modify my accent. They've also not tampered with the accents of my classmates, even though there have been surveys suggesting Scouse and Cockney accents are both pretty low down the popularity league.

Of course there are those who will tell you that changing your accent is the key to getting on in life. Research by the

Aziz Corporation found that many company directors think regional accents are a disadvantage in the world of business. But do you know who the Aziz Corporation are? (Pause) A firm of <u>image consultants</u>. Do you detect an element of vested interest here? In fairness to Mr Aziz, the company's chairman, he himself says the attitudes revealed in his survey are 'blind prejudice'.

But the evidence that regional accents are a handicap is in any case mixed to say the least. It's been reported that call centres positively favour telephone operators with regional accents. Research by Cable and Wireless has found that callers like to hear northern and Scottish accents.

In my English class at college there's the expected complement of Liverpudlians, but also Sue from Wales, Scott from Birmingham and Sarah from Newcastle. And our teacher's from Northern Ireland! I believe diversity should be celebrated, and I'm pleased that the BBC, traditionally the preserve of upper class Home Counties accents, has made a positive effort to employ presenters with regional accents.

I'm sure I speak for the great majority of young people when I say to those in charge of our education system: leave our accents alone please, they're part of what we are and we're proud of them.

Writing commentaries

Checkpoints

1 Each of these five types of imagery appeals to a different sense: visual – sight; auditory – hearing; tactile – touch; gustatory – taste; olfactory – smell.
2 A simple sentence has only one clause. A compound sentence is two simple sentences joined together by *and*, *but* or *so*.

Exam preparation

Here is a specimen commentary to accompany the earlier answer to the question on page 161:

The genre for my text is prepared speech, so it was important that I produced a text suitable for a listening audience. I am addressing a studio audience, but also a wider audience of radio listeners. I have assumed these would be people with an interest in current affairs, aged from approximately 16–17 upwards. The purpose of my talk is to persuade the audience to share my view that schools should not attempt to change pupils' accents.

As the talk is for a current affairs radio programme, the register is often quite formal. This is reflected in the use of complex lexis ('vested interest'), some of which is polysyllabic ('modify', 'diversity'). However, in order to establish a rapport with the audience much of the language used is quite informal. This includes the use of contractions ('I'm', 'you'd') and conversational expressions such as 'pretty low', 'getting on in life' and 'to say the least'.

It was important to engage the audience by speaking to them directly. I achieved this from the very beginning by the use of the second person ('If you think you have a good ear'), which continues to be a recurring feature of the text. I have also involved the audience by using interrogative sentences: 'But do you know who the Aziz Corporation are?' This question is followed by a pause, which gives greater emphasis to my answer, which also stresses the words 'image consultants'. I am making the point here that the company has a clear interest in persuading people to want to change their accents.

The inclusion of questions also helps to give the talk varied intonation, as my voice would rise when asking them. Similarly, there is an exclamatory sentence which would be delivered with a rising intonation and which I hope would produce laughter in the audience: 'And our teacher's from Northern Ireland!' Other phonological features include the use of alliteration, parallelism and tripling, which would all have a rhythmic effect: 'Sue from Wales, Scott from Birmingham and Sarah from Newcastle'.

I have begun the talk by telling the audience about my background, which I hope would engage their interest. I also make my viewpoint clear from early on. I then look critically at the case for changing pupils' accents, before presenting the opposing view. I have tried to give the talk a powerful conclusion, by ending with a strong imperative.

This chapter offers some final information and advice as you prepare for your AS or A2 exams. The first section lists and explains the **assessment objectives** used by examiners to determine your grade. Students are often unaware of these, but knowing what the examiner is looking for is clearly advantageous if you are trying to maximise your mark. There is also a checklist of literary and linguistic terms. Failure to include relevant terminology is a common failing in weaker answers. You should make sure you know these terms, and take care to use them accurately. Finally, there is a selection of 'tips for success' – some practical advice on coursework, revision and writing effective exam answers.

Exam boards

It is useful to have a copy of your exam specification. You can obtain one from the board's publications department or by downloading the specification from the board's website. The boards also supply copies of past exam papers.

→ AQA (Assessment and Qualifications Alliance)
  Publications Department, Stag Hill House, Guildford, Surrey
  GU25XJ – www.aqa.org.uk
→ EDEXCEL
  One 90 High Holborn, London WC1V 7BE –
  www.edexcel.org.uk
→ OCR (Oxford, Cambridge and Royal Society of Arts)
  1 Hills Road, Cambridge CB2 1GG – www.ocr.org.uk
→ WJEC (Welsh Joint Education Committee)
  245 Western Avenue, Cardiff CF5 2YX – www.wjec.co.uk

Topic checklist

O AS ● A2	OCR	EDEXCEL	AQA A	AQA B	WJEC
How you're assessed	O●	O●	O●	O●	O●
Terminology checklist	O●	O●	O●	O●	O●
Tips for success	O●	O●	O●	O●	O●

How you're assessed

This section outlines the structure of AS/A2 English Language and Literature courses, and how you will be assessed. In particular, it explains the eight official **assessment objectives**, which examiners use to calculate your marks.

Coursework and exams

Depending on the specification you're taking, and the options chosen by your school or college, you may be assessed by exam only or by a combination of exams and coursework. If the assessment is purely exam based, you'll probably sit three exam papers in your AS year and another three in your A2 year. If coursework is part of your assessment, you're likely to find that coursework assignments replace one AS paper and one A2 paper. Coursework (if taken) is worth 30% of the AS assessment and 30% of the A2 assessment, which means that when the marks are added together it is also worth 30% of the full A-level.

Assessment objectives

Assessment objectives (**AOs**) identify the skills and knowledge you're expected to acquire during the course. Each module usually assesses a combination of four or five objectives. Overall the objectives have a fairly equal weighting, but within individual modules the objectives will have varying degrees of importance.

It is helpful for you to know and understand the assessment objectives for the course – you are more likely to pick up marks if you know what the examiner is looking for.

Listed below are the eight assessment objectives for English Language and Literature, with a brief explanation of what each one means. Unless indicated, they are tested at both AS and A2; the difference is that at A2 a higher standard is expected.

AO1

Communicate clearly the knowledge, understanding and insights gained from the combination of literary and linguistic study, using appropriate terminology and accurate written expression.

This objective highlights your own writing skills (you need to *communicate clearly*), and also the need to know and use effectively relevant technical terms.

AO2i (AS only)

In responding to literary and non-literary texts, distinguish, describe and interpret variation in meaning and form.

This objective indicates that you will study a range of literary and non-literary texts and that you will be tested on your ability to understand their meaning and their overall structure and organisation.

Take note

As with other subjects, your AS marks account for 50% of your total A-level mark and are carried forward into your A2 year. You can though re-sit individual units (modules) before finishing the course in order to improve your final grade.

Take note

Try to find out the assessment objectives for each unit you're taking, and the weighting each objective has. For example, in the A2 synoptic module (Unit 6), you might find that AO3ii accounts for as much as 50% of the total marks.

Links

For more on what is meant by **literary and non-literary texts**, see pages 140–141.

AO2ii (A2 only)

Respond with knowledge and understanding to texts of different types and from different periods, exploring and commenting on relationships and comparisons between them.

This is similar to AO2i, but takes it further by referring specifically to texts from the past (*from different periods*), and by saying you need to show an ability to compare texts.

Take note

You are likely to compare texts at AS as well, but the ability to compare texts analytically is tested more rigorously at A2.

AO3i (AS only)

Respond to and analyse texts, using literary and linguistic concepts and approaches.

This means that you need to analyse texts from both *literary* and *linguistic* perspectives. Looking at characters and examining themes are examples of literary approaches. Linguistic approaches include, for example, the analysis of lexis and grammar.

AO3ii (A2 only)

Use and evaluate different literary and linguistic approaches to the study of written and spoken language, showing how these approaches inform their reading.

This extends AO3i by saying that at A2 you also need to explain and comment on your own methods of analysis.

AO4

Show understanding of the ways contextual variation and choices of form, style and vocabulary shape the meanings of texts.

This objective focuses on the various influences on the meaning of a text, including the context (which involves looking at elements such as genre and audience) and the way language is used.

Links

For a fuller discussion of **context**, see page 171.

AO5

Identify and consider the ways attitudes and values are created in speech and writing.

This objective refers to particular aspects of a text's meaning: the *attitudes and values* that are expressed within it. Attitudes are essentially views and opinions; values are more to do with what is considered important in life, and judgements about what is morally right or wrong.

Take note

The attitudes and values might be those of the author, or those given to characters in a literary text such as a play or novel.

AO6

Demonstrate expertise and accuracy in writing for a variety of specific purposes and audiences, drawing on knowledge of literary texts and features of language to explain and comment on the choices made.

You need to show that you can write a variety of texts, and comment analytically on your own writing.

Take note

As this objective indicates, whenever you write a text you need a clear sense of your **audience** and **purpose**. See page 155.

Terminology checklist

Here is a checklist of terms it would be useful for you to know, arranged into categories such as lexis, grammar, phonology etc. These terms are all explained elsewhere in the book (use the **Index** to find the relevant pages), and many are also in the **Glossary** that begins on page 188.

Lexis		
Word classes	Noun	Proper noun
Common noun	Concrete noun	Abstract noun
Collective noun	Adjective	Comparative
Superlative	Verb	Dynamic verb
Stative verb	Active verb	Passive verb
Adverb	Pronoun	Conjunction
Preposition	Determiner	Intensifier
Denotation	Connotation	Figurative language
Metaphor	Simile	Personification
Pathetic fallacy	Imagery	Visual imagery
Auditory imagery	Gustatory imagery	Olfactory imagery
Tactile imagery	Semantic field	Field-specific lexis
Hypernym	Hyponym	Synonym
Antonym	Contrast	Antithesis
Formal	Informal	Complex
Simple	Polysyllabic	Monosyllabic
Colloquial	Dialect vocabulary	Irony
Ambiguity	Pun	Oxymoron
Emotive	Taboo language	Euphemism
Pathos	Bathos	Jargon
Archaism	Neologism	Borrowing
Contraction	Elision	Deictic expression
Modes of address	Hyperbole	

Grammar		
Simple sentence	Compound sentence	Complex sentence
Subordinate clause	Ellipsis	Minor sentence
Declarative sentence	Interrogative sentence	Imperative sentence
Exclamatory sentence	Rhetorical question	Main verb
Auxiliary verb	Syntax	Phrase
Clause	Noun phrase	Head word
Modifier	Pre-modifier	Post-modifier
Adverbial	Foregrounding	End-focus
Inverted syntax	Parallelism	Tripling
Syndetic listing	Asyndetic listing	First person
Second person	Third person	Tense
Inflection	Non-standard grammar	Dialect grammar

Phonology		
Onomatopoeia	Rhyme	Sibilance
Dissonance	Alliteration	Half-rhyme
Assonance		

Discourse structure		
Cohesion	Anaphoric reference	Cataphoric reference
Non-linear text	Exophoric reference	Intertextual reference
Linear text		

Spoken language		
Utterance	Referential utterance	Expressive utterance
Phatic utterance	Directive utterance	Monologue
Dialogue	Disjointed construction	False start
Non-fluency features	Filler	Filled pause
Unvoiced pause	Prosodic features	Intonation
Pitch	Pace	Liaison
Juncture	Pause	Volume
Stress	Oral signal	Accent
RP accent	Transactional exchange	Interactional exchange
Adjacency pair	Three-part exchange	Topic marker
Topic shift	Topic loop	Repair
Feedback	Turn-taking	

Drama		
Plot	Sub-plot	Exposition
Complication	Resolution	Denouement
Props	Soliloquy	Dramatic irony
Aside	Naturalistic dialogue	Stylised dialogue
Hero	Protagonist	

Fiction		
Narrative viewpoint	Narrative voice	First-person narrator
Third-person narrator	Omniscient narrator	Unreliable narrator
Intrusive narrator	Unintrusive narrator	Multiple narrators
Direct speech thought	Indirect speech thought	Free direct speech
Free indirect speech		

Poetry		
Stanza	Quatrain	Refrain
Lyric poetry	Sonnet	Ode
Elegy	Narrative poetry	Epic
Ballad	Persona	Rhyme scheme
Half-rhyme	Internal rhyme	Couplet
Heroic couplet	Metre	Iambic pentameter
Blank verse	Trochaic metre	Dactylic metre
Anapaestic metre	Spondaic metre	Enjambement
Caesura		

Other terms		
Standard English	Register	Dialect
Sociolect	Idiolect	Context
Rhetorical features	Genre	Symbolism
Allegory	Old English	Middle English
Early Modern English	Late Modern English	